D1413606

School Systems
THAT LEARN

WITHDRAWAL

*I want to thank my family for giving me love,
support, and guidance throughout the writing
process, and my colleagues for helping me clarify
my thinking. I also want to thank Stephanie Hirsh of
Learning Forward, who encouraged me to share
my story on how to develop and nurture
ongoing educator capacity building that
improves learning for ALL students.*

—Paul B. Ash

*I would like to thank all the educators and
students that I have had the good fortune to work
with since 1971. What I have learned from them
cannot be adequately measured.*

—John D'Auria

School Systems

THAT LEARN

Improving Professional Practice,
Overcoming Limitations,
and Diffusing Innovation

PAUL B. ASH ○ JOHN D'AURIA

A Joint Publication

LB
2822.8
.A84
2013

HARVARD UNIVERSITY
GRADUATE SCHOOL OF EDUCATION
MONROE C. GUTMAN LIBRARY

CORWIN
A SAGE Company

FOR INFORMATION:

Corwin

A SAGE Company

2455 Teller Road

Thousand Oaks, California 91320

(800) 233-9936

www.corwin.com

SAGE Publications Ltd.

1 Oliver's Yard

55 City Road

London EC1Y 1SP

United Kingdom

SAGE Publications India Pvt. Ltd.

B 1/I 1 Mohan Cooperative Industrial Area

Mathura Road, New Delhi 110 044

India

SAGE Publications Asia-Pacific Pte. Ltd.

3 Church Street

#10-04 Samsung Hub

Singapore 049483

Acquisitions Editor: Dan Alpert

Associate Editor: Kimberly Greenberg

Editorial Assistant: Heidi Arndt

Production Editor: Amy Schroller

Copy Editor: Alan Cook

Typesetter: C&M Digitals (P) Ltd.

Proofreader: Jennifer Thompson

Indexer: Jean Casalegno

Cover Designer: Rose Storey

Graphic Designer: Cristina Kubota

Permissions Editor: Karen Ehrmann

Copyright © 2013 by Corwin

All rights reserved. When forms and sample documents are included, their use is authorized only by educators, local school sites, and/or noncommercial or nonprofit entities that have purchased the book. Except for that usage, no part of this book may be reproduced or utilized in any form or by any means, electronic or mechanical, including photocopying, recording, or by any information storage and retrieval system, without permission in writing from the publisher.

Printed in the United States of America

A catalog record of this book is available from the Library of Congress.

ISBN 9781452271989

This book is printed on acid-free paper.

12 13 14 15 16 10 9 8 7 6 5 4 3 2 1

Contents

About the Authors

Paul B. Ash, PhD, has served as superintendent of the Lexington, Massachusetts Public Schools since 2005. Previously, he served as the superintendent of schools in the Westwood, Massachusetts Public Schools from 1998 to 2005. He has also held the following positions in the Wellesley, Massachusetts Public Schools: Director of Professional Personnel and Staff Development; Assistant Superintendent for Personnel, Finance, and Administration; Assistant Superintendent for Personnel and Planning; and Interim Superintendent of Schools. He started his career in education as a chemistry, physics, and earth science teacher at the Dover-Sherborn Regional High School in Dover, Massachusetts.

Dr. Ash received the doctor of philosophy degree from Boston College, the Certificate of Advanced Graduate Study from Harvard University's Graduate School of Education, the Master of Arts in Teaching degree from the University of Massachusetts, and the Bachelor of Science degree in chemistry from Worcester Polytechnic Institute. He has served Boston College as an adjunct faculty member, providing instruction in educational finance and facilities management to masters and doctoral students. He is currently a member of the National Superintendents Roundtable and has served on the National Board of Governors for the American Association of School Administrators.

John D'Auria, EdD, moved from directing the Canton, Massachusetts Public Schools as superintendent to becoming president of Teachers21, a nonprofit organization working to ensure that all school-aged children are given an equal opportunity to succeed by endeavoring to provide them with educators who are eminently knowledgeable and qualified to teach them.

In a career that has spanned four decades as a math teacher, guidance counselor, principal, and superintendent, Dr. D'Auria has worked with hundreds of school leaders around sharpening the academic focus of school teams, developing a vibrant school culture, and managing conflict in the workplace.

Dr. D'Auria's research focuses on the ways in which the assumptions that people hold about intelligence significantly influence their learning. His newest book is *Ten Lessons in Leadership and Learning* (2010). He is also the author of "The DNA of Leadership"—a curriculum for aspiring school leaders in the Massachusetts Leadership Licensure Program—and coauthor with Jon Saphier of *How to Bring Vision to School Improvement* (Research for Better Teaching, 1993). Numerous other articles include "The Superintendent as Teacher" (*Phi Delta Kappan* Online Edition, Fall, 2009); "A Principal's Dilemma" (jointly with Matt King in *Schools: Studies in Education*, Spring, 2009); and "Three Strands Form Strong School Leadership" (jointly with Jon Saphier and Matt King, *Journal of Staff Development*, Spring, 2006). He is a frequent speaker at national and regional educational conferences and has served on The Middle School Curriculum Project based at Education Development Center, Waltham, MA.

John D'Auria is a Phi Beta Kappa and summa cum laude graduate of Boston College, where he majored in mathematics and philosophy; he earned his doctorate in urban educational leadership at the University of Massachusetts.

Introduction

Transformation

Moving a School District Into a Learning System

A seasoned educator has just become the new superintendent of a district that has 3,100 students in one preschool, three elementary schools, one middle school, and one high school. About 10% of the families qualify for free and reduced lunch, and the quickly changing student population is about 20% students of color. For the past five years, the town government did not have sufficient funds to match the rising costs of contractual obligations, special education, utilities, and health benefits. The increases in these budget areas often averaged 4% to 10% annually, while the school revenues remained constant or increased by 1% to 2%. This yearly gap between revenues and costs frequently resulted in staff reductions and program eliminations.

Most recently, the district eliminated 22 positions, and class sizes approached 30 students in most elementary classes. Families were burdened with a $400 fee for bus transportation and nearly $300 per sport for students to participate in high school athletics. There also were fees for student drivers to park their cars ($150), for elementary students to participate in an after-school play ($50), and for middle school students to enjoy after-school activities ($100).

The middle school had so few enrichment courses that the one remaining art teacher had over 600 students. In order to fill the holes left in the schedule from staff reductions, study halls multiplied, with the largest containing 120 students during the lunch block. This "study hall" was in the gymnasium, where young adolescents sat on the gym floor for the period.

The funding gap also affected contract negotiations. Five different union contracts expired right before the superintendent started. In order to prevent further staff reductions, the school board couldn't offer a cost-of-living increase

> *to teachers, custodians, secretaries, or food service workers. Morale was low, particularly among the custodians, who manned a picket line because the school committee was considering outsourcing their jobs. In the face of such a stark outlook, many veteran administrators and teachers retired early, and the new superintendent had to hire three principals, five department chairs, and a director of curriculum, instruction, and technology. This represented a significant upheaval for a relatively small district.*
>
> *One of the schools in the district was placed in corrective action by the Department of Education because it had not met its adequate yearly progress (AYP) scores for several consecutive years.*

Reprinted with permission of Phi Delta Kappa International, www.pdkintl.org. All rights reserved.

This real scenario (D'Auria, 2009) contains elements that are typical of the problems that confront superintendents in small, medium, and large districts. And while there are no easy formulas or guaranteed approaches to ensure a successful turnaround, the process will nonetheless resemble the efforts and interventions of skillful teachers working with students in their classrooms. Similarly to a teacher, the superintendent will have to apply good instruction, personal relationship building, collaborative inquiry, careful planning, best practices, and dispassionate examination of the data. And, like any good teacher, the superintendent needs to *check for understanding* and, where warranted, reteach.

Superintendents need to convey lots of information to a variety of constituencies. Most members of these groups (parents, taxpayers, and elected officials) do not have a background in education, though they all experienced school. In the scenario outlined above, increased funding was clearly the district's most daunting and most pressing need. While there is no doubt that efficiencies could be found in the budget, the schools needed more money. The superintendent discovered that a recent ballot initiative to raise taxes to gain additional revenue for the schools lost by only 300 votes. Further examination showed that a number of parents had not voted in that election. Why was that? An initial hypothesis was that not enough parents were invested in the state of the schools. However, results of focus groups showed that there was not a shared understanding of the hallmarks of a quality school system. Interviews with various town constituents led the superintendent to realize that significant animosity and mistrust existed among and between stakeholder groups. From this new data, the superintendent and his educational team shifted their strategy from one that just focused on getting out the vote to a three-step action plan:

1. Establish forums where community members can air their different perspectives openly and respectfully,

2. Provide multiple opportunities for community members to learn about the educational issues facing the schools, and

3. Publicize criteria used in university research to assess the quality of education within a district.

One strategy the superintendent utilized, as a result of this new thinking, was to *teach* the *curriculum* of the budget by translating it into lessons that would engage the audience and bring about an understanding of the important ideas, rather than simply convey information. For example, due to budgetary constraints, elementary class sizes were exceeding 30 students. The superintendent realized that a simple graph showing the data would not help those community members who experienced class sizes of 40 or 50 students when they were in elementary school to understand the problems posed by large class sizes today.

Trying to explain how special education costs affect the school budget requires teaching minilessons on state and federal mandates, explaining autism and its very dramatic increase in school populations, and explaining why inclusion is worthwhile although it requires more initial expense. To *teach* about class size, the superintendent wrote an article for the local newspaper. With it, he included a class photo from his own elementary school years and asked:

Can you spot the future superintendent of Canton in this 1959 photo of my 4th-grade class? There are 61 students who were part of my classroom that year. Given the fact that I was able to attain an advanced degree and gain a leadership position, one can easily conclude that such a large class size did little to limit my ability to succeed in school and ultimately secure a reasonable job. While this is a logical conclusion, as an educator, I must also point out that not everyone benefited from this one-size-fits-all model that allowed class sizes to be this large. If you look "behind the scenes" of this photo, you will not be able to detect anyone with a learning disability or with special needs. If students had such needs, they would not have been able to be part of this class. They would have had to attend a special school or be educated at home. If you happen to be one of the girls in this class, your career options would be limited to the basic three: homemaker, teacher, or nurse. You also would have had little opportunity to play organized sports. Also absent from this photo are any nonwhite faces. Again, if you happened to be a person of color, you more than likely would have had to attend a different school. I mention these "exceptions" because we often remember fondly the benefits of a previous era of schooling, while not viewing the limitations that also existed during this time. Education was not as adaptive and responsive to the range of needs and backgrounds that we are currently responsible to meet and support.

While I am proud of the progress we have made in the field of education over the past half a century, I know that our expanded expectations require a different model than the "one size fits all." We expect and demand from our teachers more personalization, communication, and attention to individual needs. In order to accomplish this, class sizes must be within reasonable limits.

As the superintendent in this case began to convey these *lessons* about the school district, some stakeholders reacted with strong arguments against more funds going to the schools. Some of their statements were caustic. Because of what the superintendent and his team had learned earlier about the corrosive effects of mistrust and anger, the superintendent responded to the critiques in a calm and dispassionate manner, recognizing that the tone of his responses was just as critical as the content of his words. Dispassionate responses to vitriolic critiques began to shift the tenor of the exchanges in the newspaper. Additionally, because of what his team learned from community forums, instead of avoiding those who opposed increased funding, team members reached out to those who had conflicting views. This collaborative approach that engaged the community in a learning cycle led to a political victory that increased funding for the schools.

The story offers one example of how a leader should operate within a learning school system to bridge differences and build a shared understanding of the challenges and goals of the district. While the specifics will differ in each case, educators who utilize a learning cycle that nimbly responds to the root causes of a problem raise the likelihood of achieving success.

Every adult member of a learning school system demonstrates learning, teaching, and collaboration. While there are distinct and specific roles and focus points for each employee—finance officer, director, coach, assistant principal, department head, teacher, paraprofessional, and others—all adult members of the system play the roles of learners, collaborators, and teachers within their distinct job responsibilities, asking questions, collecting data, facilitating teamwork, implementing strategies, assessing impact, and, where necessary, recycling through these phases until goals are achieved.

A LEARNING SCHOOL SYSTEM SHIFTS THE WORK FROM THE INDIVIDUAL TO THE TEAM

Every school district strives to serve all its students well. The capacity of the district to ensure that every individual student learns the skills, knowledge, and dispositions that represent excellence is traditionally thought of as a function of the abilities of individual teachers and principals. It is our contention that the capacity of a school district to provide all students with a gold-standard education is directly proportional to the system's ability to function as a learning unit. The more that teachers, principals, and central office staff act as individuals rather than as members of a collective whole, the less likely that all students will be educated well. As marketing consultant Simon Sinek points out, "Success always takes help. Failure you can do alone." Sinek continues in a recent blog post,

> There is something to be said for being the smartest or the most talented one in the room . . . too bad it doesn't help much in reality. Success, by any definition, is a team sport. I learned this little detail the hard way. There was a time in my life that I thought that if I wanted to make anything out of myself, I'd be responsible for all of it by myself. I thought I could do everything primarily because I thought I should do everything. I needed to know how to be the boss, the accountant, the creative director, the marketing manager, the HR director, set the strategy and do the work with my clients. Even if I hired or worked with others, I wanted to be the final say on everything. This was a brilliant strategy until three things happened.
>
> 1. I learned I wasn't good at everything
> 2. I didn't have the energy to do everything
> 3. I failed
>
> The human animal is a social animal and our survival and success depend on our ability to find communities of people who share our values and beliefs. When these communities form, trust emerges. It is then that the human animal will adapt from a survival instinct by self-preservation to one of working for the good of the community. Both are designed to help the individual survive, but it is the community that has the greater chance of not only survival but success. (2010)

FRACTALS—A MODEL FOR UNDERSTANDING THE SELF-SIMILARITIES OF A LEARNING SCHOOL SYSTEM

What is a fractal? A fractal is "a rough or fragmented geometric shape that can be split into parts, each of which is (at least approximately) a reduced-size copy of the whole," (Mandelbrot, 1982) or in other words, a geometric shape which exhibits *self-similarity*. The term *fractal* was coined by Benoît Mandelbrot in 1975 and was derived from the Latin *fractus*, meaning "broken" or "fractured" (Fractals, n.d.).

A fractal repeats itself at smaller and larger scales. If one takes a head of broccoli and removes one floret, the small part will resemble the whole. If one removes a portion of the floret, the part again resembles the original section. In a learning school system, the learning dynamic that occurs between a student and a teacher is replicated among teachers and principals, and further mirrored in the work among and between central office staff and building principals. In such a school system, no matter where one looks, the pattern is the same.

In learning school systems, this symmetry is not a function of gene activation (as it is in broccoli) but rather is the result of intentional and informed leadership. The symmetry provides improved coordination and a reduction in lost energy due to weak organization of efforts.

Leveraging the potential of the whole system acting in a coordinated set of efforts gives access to energies that often go untapped in school districts that rely more heavily on the capacities and abilities of individual educators. In a *learning school system*, the whole is greater than the sum of the parts. The late inventor Buckminster Fuller referred to this dynamic as *synergy*, which he defined as "a behavior of a whole system unpredicted by the behavior of its parts taken separately." Noted educator Michael Fullan describes this synergy as the organization's *collective capacity*: "The collective ability, dispositions, skills, knowledge, motivation, and resources—to act together to bring about positive change. That is what is called for to sustain continuous improvement" (Fullan, 2005).

The Learning Cycle

In a learning school system, learning cycles are replicated in each and every aspect of the institution. A learning cycle consists of the following phases:

1. Study a problem.

2. Investigate a range of potential strategies. Examine locally and externally researched interventions.

3. Experiment with a particular strategy or combination of strategies.

4. Examine and evaluate the data that result from the experimentation.

5. If an acceptable solution is not achieved, the learner returns to Step 3 and adjusts the original methodology or creates a new strategy as a result of the analysis of the data in Step 4.

In a learning school system, this pattern may be observed at the student level in a student or team of students in a science class trying to determine the nature of the components in a beaker filled with sludge.

At the teacher level, this pattern may be observed in a professional learning community as a group of teachers try to improve the effectiveness of their strategies to teach students division of fractions.

At the school level, this pattern may be observed as principals work together to examine the effectiveness of their strategies to implement a new approach to literacy.

At the central office level, this pattern may be observed in the way district leaders examine their attempts to close the achievement gaps.

At the school board level, this pattern may be observed in the manner in which the school board and superintendent deal with an unexpected environmental crisis affecting a local elementary school.

Professional development in a learning school system is comprised of course work and coaching designed to strengthen teacher practice and to address student learning needs. After each course, data are collected to examine whether the new pedagogical approaches or curricular developments are implemented properly and are successful at achieving desired results. If they are not successful, the professional development plan is revised to address where the interventions broke down.

At any meeting in a learning school system, members address a student learning issue by first examining data from multiple sources. One would hear a robust conversation where participants actively challenge each other's thinking; out of that conflict would emerge a commitment to a plan of intervention that, at a later meeting, would have to pass the test of having achieved measurable results. This would be characteristic of meetings that occurred within schools as well as between schools.

The cycle above not only achieves solutions to problems, but it also continually adds "local" knowledge to the collective skill base of practitioners. The individual, the group, the team, and ultimately the system continually improve by adding new knowledge through each of the learning cycles. This collective learning is not limited to academic dimensions. In a learning system, the approach to every challenge and every problem is to study and analyze the context, develop solutions, collect data, and extract from it insights that inform the next round of strategic work until an effective solution is achieved. Ineffective problem resolutions lead to further experimentation. Whether the issue is removing an environmental hazard from a local elementary school, improving participation rates in AP courses, strategizing about how to strengthen differentiated instruction, examining a more cost-effective approach to deliver special education services, or mounting a community campaign to gain support for an increase in taxes that fund local schools, the educators within a learning school system approach their work collaboratively and analytically, constantly distilling the learning that is acquired even from failed attempts and less than desired results. In such a school system, the constant modeling of how to approach problem solving is an overarching benefit to students and staff alike. In the words of noted educator Michael Fullan "learning is the work" (2008b, p. 75).

While learning occurs in most schools, it happens in a disorganized and isolated manner and without the benefit of systemic support. Results are not necessarily documented or shared, and the focus is often at the individual level. Teachers often work independently of each other; in addition, principals are isolated or in competitive situations. The work of the central office is often seen as disconnected from, or at odds with, the work "on the ground." We will argue in this text that learning can be enhanced when educators make explicit efforts to implement the learning cycle in all processes, meetings, and system behaviors. These efforts will increase the probability that every student will achieve a high-quality education, because the efforts of the whole system will be harnessed to achieve goals. Loss of energy and focus through personnel changes will be minimized, and the repeated modeling will help ensure that an important goal will be achieved: continual learning. In a learning school system, student achievement is viewed not just as the responsibility of individual teachers acting alone, but also as the responsibility of the school and the school system. There is a relentless striving for more effective solutions, based on a constant examination and reexamination of the systems that contribute to results. The benefits of becoming a learning system are

- more long-term sustainability, because the learning capacity of the system blunts the impact of staff turnover;
- increased opportunities for teachers to expand their skills and proficiencies as a result of collaboration between schools and districtwide professional development aligned with school and district goals;
- improved capacity-building opportunities for administrators through collegial support;
- effective use of limited district funds; and

- more programs for students than individual schools can offer (for example, special education programs and magnet programs for all students).

RECYCLING MISTAKES INTO LEARNING

While many embrace the concept of continued learning, advocates do so without adequately recognizing how messy, uncomfortable, and discouraging the learning cycle can be at times. It will often involve making mistakes, failure, and engaging in conflict. And while failure cannot be acceptable, it is often a temporary way station on the road to goal attainment. Sir Kenneth Robinson points out in his TED video "Are Schools Killing Creativity?" that we are now creating school systems that are overly influenced by test results, and consequently "mistakes are the worst thing you can make." Robinson clarifies that making mistakes is not the same as being creative, but if one "is not prepared to be wrong, one will never come up with anything original." (2006).

It is for these reasons that one of the most vital components of a learning school system is the ability of its leaders to develop learning climates that foster continual experimentation with new strategies and ideas to improve student learning. Experimentation, however, also brings with it mistakes, setbacks, false starts, and less-than-satisfactory results. If mistakes like these are consistently viewed as signs of weakness or something to be avoided at all costs, the inquiry and honest analysis required of *learners* within this framework will be impeded. The test for the health of a learning system climate is what occurs when results are not achieved after implementing a set of strategies. If the system responds with punitive measures, then the relentless reexamination of results and a recrafting of interventions until the desired goals are achieved will often be replaced by camouflage, blame, avoidance, and less-than-forthright assessments.

In essence, this cycle of applying strategies, examining results, and rethinking one's original hypothesis is what is expected of teachers working with students. It is also the most important habit of mind to instill in our students. Students in a learning school system would enter the learning process with the belief that anything is possible to master if one is willing to analyze, experiment, honestly review the result of one's efforts and strategies, and start the cycle all over again by shifting strategies and increasing efforts until one has mastered the skill or understood the concept. This is what social psychologist Carol Dweck refers to as a *growth mindset* (Dweck, 2008). Encouraging this kind of approach to learning, and in particular, this view of mistakes, is dependent upon a very critical ingredient: feedback loops.

Feedback Loops

A feedback loop may be illustrated by an analogy to a computer game: feedback is rapid, specific, and nonjudgmental.

There is no penalty for those who need to try it a second, third, or fourth time in order to get it right. The feedback is immediate and ongoing. The player also knows *along the way* how he or she is doing. The feedback is user friendly. It's clear, specific, and useful to the performer. The quality of the feedback promotes self-directed learning (as opposed to learning imposed from someone who tells the participant what to do) because the *player* uses the feedback to self-adjust. The criteria for success are clearly spelled out. The ability of a school system to create these kinds of feedback loops for students, teachers, and administrators is a critical aspect of a learning school system.

Providing timely and ongoing feedback requires attending to data flow structures, scheduling meetings that bring data and people together, and creating a system that is firm on goal attainment but lenient on students when they don't learn on their first attempt. The belief exhibited in such a school system is: *It will take time and multiple attempts before excellence is achieved.*

EFFECTIVE COLLABORATION

Another vital aspect of the culture within a vibrant learning school system is effective collaboration that shows up in every domain and aspect of the system. The insights on teamwork developed by nationally renowned experts in professional learning communities, Rick and Becky DuFour, have helped us to understand that when educators work collaboratively rather than in isolation, students learn more (Dufour & Eaker, 1998).

Dufour and Eaker define effective collaboration in professional learning communities as follows:

- Shared vision and values that lead to a collective commitment of school staff, which is expressed in day-to-day practices;
- Solutions actively sought, openness to new ideas;
- Working teams cooperate to achieve common goals;
- Encouragement of experimentation as an opportunity to learn;
- Questioning of the status quo, leading to an ongoing quest for improvement and professional learning;
- Continuous improvement based on an evaluation of outcomes rather than on the intentions expressed; and
- Reflection in order to study the operation and impacts of actions taken.

The functioning of teams in a school system offers a window to examine how effectively that system embraces collaboration. Are teams valued, nurtured, developed, and supported? In a learning school system, teams are the unit of study, and the concept of *team* applies not only to collections of individuals but also to groups and schools within the system. If there is more than one school at a particular level (elementary, middle, high), the expectation is that collaboration will occur between and among schools as frequently as it occurs within schools.

REVISIONING CONFLICT—EMBRACING IT AS THE PRECURSOR TO COMMITMENT

Effective collaboration is built upon the capacity of educators to engage in and resolve conflict. Conflict can be particularly challenging when competing perspectives and values require a range of communication skills to untangle. Educators often lack these vital communication skills. Additionally, educators can often be averse to conflict. D'Auria and King write about this gap in educator preparation:

> One of the great mysteries of our profession is why so little is done to prepare aspiring teachers, and especially school administrators, for the conflict that occurs in schools. Conflict with students, parents, colleagues, and supervisors is what wakes us up in the middle of the night with a pit in our stomach. Difficult conversations that have gone bad, are being avoided, or which will take place the next day grip our minds, dominate our self-talk, drain our emotional energy, and block us from being more present-centered. While there are technical bodies of knowledge that must be learned, far too little emphasis is placed on the emotional capacities that contribute to effective leadership. (2009, p. 132)

TRUST—A CRITICAL FACTOR IN CREATING A CLIMATE OF CONTINUAL IMPROVEMENT

Learning how to manage conflict, recycle mistakes into learning, and dispassionately examine results until desired goals are achieved requires an enormous amount of trust. By trust, we are not referring simply to a positive feeling that one can rely on colleagues or leaders; rather, we mean the ability of members of the *system* to admit their vulnerability, to ask for assistance, and to be able to learn and acquire new proficiencies over time.

Trust is one crucial quality of the pattern that is repeated at all levels of the learning school system "fractal." Within a single classroom, a skilled teacher engenders trust—or the ability of her students to admit their vulnerability as learners—by how she communicates beliefs, handles mistakes, and builds relationships with students. A principal develops a climate of trust—or the ability of the staff to admit their vulnerability as learners—in a similar manner. A superintendent in a learning school system would also build a climate of trust as defined by the ability of principals to ask for assistance.

SHIFTING ARCHITECTURE OF SCHOOLS

In a learning system, teachers see their roles more as architects of learning experiences for their students than as conveyers of information. Principals in such a dynamic system see themselves less as building managers, chief disciplinarians, and overseers and more like leaders who shape and influence learning cultures for teachers. Central office leaders in a learning school system continue to think about budgets, politics, and school board relationships—*and* they also see their most significant work as supporting and inspiring the learning and efforts of principals. As with more traditional architecture, blueprints that illustrate details are necessary as is an inspiring vision within a framework that contains costs. Currently, schools are built to maintain the status quo rather than to adjust to the ever-changing needs of students in ways that will achieve desired results. In the ensuing chapters, the authors share their insights on how to transform a school district from a rigid architecture comprised of individuals to one that is characterized by flexibility, responsiveness, collaboration, and synergy.

OUTLINE OF THE BOOK

In the following chapters, the authors will explore the dimensions of a K–12 learning school system designed to create a culture of innovation and diffusion of best practices from small groups of educators to educators throughout a school system. Chapters 1 and 2 describe how the current paradigm of education limits school systems in their ability to teach all students at high levels and how school systems can overcome these obstacles. Chapter 1 describes the current dominant model of education, the origins of this model, and its limitations. We examine 200 years of U.S. education history and discuss six historical factors that limit a school system's capacity to educate all students. This chapter shows how teacher isolation, overstandardization, and a narrow view of professional development limits a school's or school system's ability to solve education problems and to develop more effective instructional practices.

Chapter 2 presents a new paradigm of whole school system change that can overcome the limitations of the past, close achievement gaps, raise academic achievement for all students, and unleash educator potential to create lasting cultural change in their schools and school systems from a compliance and standardization model to a collaborative learning organization. We introduce four drivers of change that, when working synergistically, will unleash teacher creativity to develop new educational solutions for all students.

Chapters 3 through 6 describe the four drivers of a K–12 learning school system in more depth: the importance of trust, collaboration in all directions, capacity building for all educators, and leadership at all levels. Without these components, teachers retreat to their classrooms and work less effectively in teams. In Chapter 3, we discuss the importance of building and sustaining a climate of trust and how to repair trust when it is broken. In Chapter 4, we examine how a district must move from a collection of individuals to a collaborative enterprise. In Chapter 5, we discuss the traditional model of teacher professional development and why schools need to adopt new ways to expand individual, school, and systemwide educator capacity. In Chapter 6, we discuss the importance of developing leaders at all levels of a school system, in order to expand school and district capacity to educate all students at higher levels.

Chapters 7 and 8 discuss what school leaders can do to overcome a variety of obstacles to change coming from colleagues, school administrators, elected officials, parents, and unions. In Chapter 7, we carefully examine the various constituencies that may block changes within a school or school system and why these constituencies may resist change. In Chapter 8, we offer a method for overcoming these obstacles to change and present a model, adapted from more than 60 years of research, for diffusing innovation throughout a school or school system. The model shows how school leaders can support the development of new ideas, help colleagues work through resistance, and support these colleagues with professional development as they learn and adopt new practices of teaching and learning.

1

Six Reasons Why School Systems Don't Educate All Students at High Levels

Imagine that you are the superintendent of schools in a highly respected school district. Your K–12 school district is well funded, has great teachers, and has strong community support. The vast majority of students perform extremely well on all state and national examinations. However, there are still significant achievement gaps within your school system.

Why do these achievement gaps continue to exist, even in well-funded school districts? Why can't these K–12 school districts close the achievement gap?

There are three potential responses:

1. It's not possible for all students to achieve at high levels;

2. Our work has not been successful, so we just need to keep adding more achievement gap initiatives; or

3. The K–12 organization, as designed, has reached the limits of its capacity and needs to be changed to ensure more students achieve at high levels.

It's Not Possible for All Students to Achieve at High Levels

We know the first hypothesis is not true for individual schools. In the book *It's Being Done: Academic Success in Unexpected Schools*, Karin Chenoweth describes 15 individual schools in the United States that closed or nearly closed achievement gaps between poor children and children of color with white and Asian children (2007, p. 11). In each chapter of her book, she describes the demographics of the rural, suburban, and city schools she studied and what each school did to reach proficiency rates into the 80% or 90% range or to demonstrate "sustained and rapid improvement over multiple years" (p. 11). In addition, the Education Trust lists on its web site 25 schools where more than 50% of its students are poor and performed in the top 25% in the state. These achievement gap success stories were selected as part of a program called *Dispelling the Myth* ("Success stories," 2012).

Our Work Has Not Been Successful, So We Just Need to Keep Adding More Achievement Gap Initiatives

During at least the last two decades, school districts all across the United States have tried initiative after initiative to close the achievement gap for students. A Google search on the term *achievement gap* showed 1,600,000 results on July 11, 2011. A review of the first 900 articles reveals a wide range of achievement gap initiatives tried by different schools. None of the articles claimed that entire K–12 school districts were able to close the achievement gaps for students of color and white students. When the Google search was narrowed to *African American achievement gap*, there were 846,000 results on July 10, 2011. When the search was narrowed to *Hispanic achievement gap* on the same date, there were 896,000 results.

In 2008, a study was conducted by Vito LaMura, the retired president of the Lexington, Massachusetts teachers' association, who verified significant racial achievement gaps in eight relatively wealthy, high-performing school districts in the Boston area (LaMura, 2007). For more than 10 years, the eight school districts implemented a wide range of initiatives to raise academic achievement for their students of color as part of a 43-year voluntary integration program known as METCO. In 1966, the Massachusetts legislature established the Metropolitan Council for Educational Opportunity (METCO) to expand educational opportunities, increase diversity, and reduce racial isolation, by permitting students in Boston and Springfield to attend public schools in other communities that have agreed to participate.

Given that these school districts were engaged in significant efforts to close the achievement gap for more than a decade, why did their achievement gaps persist? We do not believe it was from a lack of initiatives.

Some of the area superintendents have suggested the following potential reasons for failure: the focus was on the wrong drivers of change, the change process was not systemic K through 12, and there was lack of deep implementation with fidelity.

The Organization, as Designed, Has Reached the Limits of Its Capacity and Needs to Be Changed to Ensure More Students Achieve at High Levels

In this book, we will explore why the vast majority of schools in the United States have not been able to get "all students across the finish line" (that is, to have all students demonstrating proficiency in the core curriculum). While we acknowledge that there are some incompetently run school systems, we believe that most school systems provide the best education that they are designed to produce. Teachers and administrators come to work every day and do the best job they know how to do. However, we believe that most school systems, as they are currently designed, have reached the limits of their capacity.

Before diving into this problem, the following analogy may help explain our point of view more clearly.

Why can't a six-year-old boy run a four-minute mile? There are two problems. First, even with a huge breakfast (more energy), his biological system cannot convert the food energy into usable energy fast enough. Second, even if his metabolic system could generate enough energy per second, his body is not designed to produce enough mechanical energy for his legs to run fast enough. Therefore, even if this child ate just the right foods every day and exercised every day, he could never run a four-minute mile.

We argue that current school systems were never designed to ensure all students achieve at high levels. Built into the design is a structure that does not allow sufficient resources and focus to produce high educational achievement for all students. For more than 200 years, American schools were designed to educate only some students. Beginning in the 1960s, the courts and legislatures began to insist that schools must educate everyone. Only recently in our country's history are we striving to educate all students at high levels.

Before presenting our ideas to improve learning for all students within a K–12 school system, we will begin our story with a brief history of American schools. This story partially explains why the current structures of school systems limit our ability to teach all students at high levels. While our forefathers designed and created schools that met the needs of some Americans, years ago schools were not designed to educate all Americans. The history of how American schools were organized provides clues as to why even the highest-performing American schools today cannot close the achievement gap.

In this chapter, we identify six historical factors, excluding financial limitations, which have limited the capacity of school systems to educate all students at high levels. Each of the limitations will be discussed from a historical perspective. The six limitations are

1. Laws and regulations: Schools are designed for some students, not all students

2. Mindsets and limiting beliefs about learning

3. Standardization versus differentiation

4. Teacher isolation versus teacher collaboration, leadership, and engagement

5. A narrow view of professional development

6. Teaching and student learning as separate acts, not as an interactive process

School leaders must understand the major systemic, organizational, and cultural limitations on a school's capacity to educate all students at high levels before these limitations can be overcome. The remainder of this book describes how to break the limitations of the past and increase the capacity of educators to overcome obstacles, teach all students at high levels, and diffuse innovations and best practices throughout both individual schools and school systems.

LIMITATION ONE: LAWS AND REGULATIONS

Schools Are Designed for Some Students, Not All Students

Education as we know it in America today exists within a complex network of federal and state laws and regulations. These laws, enacted and amended over the years, reflect the values and social policy of the people who held power at the time those laws were created and amended, in the jurisdictions in which those laws have effect. These laws and regulations created rights and benefits for some and limitations, obstacles, and barriers for others.

Over the last 200 years, not only have laws, institutions, and legal frameworks changed, but the role of government in education has changed significantly. At the time of the American Revolution, education was the responsibility of local cities and towns. Over the years, states gradually took more and more responsibility for educating children, using tax revenue to finance education and placing licensure requirements upon teachers. In the 1950s through the 1970s, the federal government took on new roles and responsibilities in the education of children, removing some legal barriers to education access for certain groups and setting education policy for the coming years.

At the time of the American Revolution, our forefathers did not envision a nation that needed to or should educate all people. Education was a privilege for children whose parents could afford to pay for their education, and mostly for boys. In this section, we briefly summarize 200 years of history that shows that public schools in the United States were not designed to educate all students at high levels. Until very recently in our history, most Americans believed that only some students should be educated at high levels.

In the late 1700s, Thomas Jefferson embraced the vision that all white male and female children be educated by the state. He proclaimed, "If a nation expects to be ignorant and free, it expects what never was and never will be." Jefferson believed that the "common man" could elect wise leaders if the populace was educated.

To further his vision, in 1778 Jefferson asked the Virginia legislature to approve his Bill for the More General Diffusion of Knowledge. Although his bill never successfully passed the legislature, Jefferson proposed that the state establish elementary schools with a curriculum that taught

> reading, writing, and common arithmetick, and the books which shall be used therein for instructing the children to read shall be such as will at the same time make them acquainted with Graecian, Roman, English, and American history. (cited in Dorn, 2012)

The bill, had it passed, would have entitled these children to three years of education paid for entirely by the state, and three more years at private expense. By "all the free children," Jefferson meant whites only.

In 1789, Massachusetts was the first state to use tax revenue to finance public education, though only for white children and only in some towns. Even as the state financing of public education grew, most schools remained racially segregated. In the 1800s, southern states began to pass laws outlawing the education of blacks. For example, in 1831 the Virginia legislature passed a law making it illegal to educate blacks.

> Be it further enacted, That if any white person assembles with free negroes or mulattos, at any school-house, church, meeting-house, or other place for the purpose of instructing such free negroes or mulattoes to read or write, such person or persons shall, on conviction thereof, be fined a sum not exceeding fifty dollars, and moreover may be imprisoned at the discretion of a jury, not exceeding two months. Be it further enacted, That if any white person, for pay or

compensation, shall assemble with any slaves for the purpose of teaching, and shall teach any slave to read or write, such person, or any white person or persons contracting with such teacher so to act, who shall offend as aforesaid, shall, for each offence, be fined at the discretion of a jury, in a sum not less than ten, not exceeding one hundred dollars. ("Legal Status," 1871)

Following Thomas Jefferson's vision to educate the "common man," Horace Mann of Massachusetts became the first state Secretary of Education in the country in 1837. He espoused state education for all children, and his views were very controversial. He was fiercely antislavery, against corporal punishment, and believed that schools must be nonsectarian. Mann believed that

universal education would be the "great equalizer" of human conditions, the "balance wheel of social machinery," and the "creator of wealth undreamed of." Poverty would most assuredly disappear as a broadening popular intelligence tapped new treasures of natural and material wealth. Along with poverty would go the rancorous discord between the "haves" and the "have nots" which had characterized all human history. Crime would decline sharply, as would a host of moral vices like intemperance, cupidity, licentiousness, violence and fraud. The ravages of ill health would certainly abate. In sum, there was no end to the social good which might be derived from a common school. (Cremin, 1957, pp. 8–9)

Horace Mann was unusual for his time and for decades after his death. As late as 1912, for example, Edward Thorndike, who was elected president of the American Psychological Association and was one of the most influential educators in the early 20th century, challenged the progressive notion that schools should educate everyone. Thorndike, a proponent of Social Darwinism said, "Even to-day such an ideal for the education of the three quarters of a million children in New York City's schools seems a little absurd" (Thorndike, 1914, p. 33). He believed that "it would be wasteful of time to train Jews and Negroes identically" (p. 32).

The issue of which races had the right to attend schools was fiercely debated in the State of California in the 1880s and 1890s. On April 7, 1880, the Legislature repealed the California Political Code, Sections 1669, 1670, and 1671, enacted in 1869–1870, which had mandated separate schools for white children and for African American and Indian children, except where the school trustees "fail to provide" such separate schools. However, in 1885, permission to establish racially segregated schools was restored; the Legislature passed an amendment to Political Code 1662 stating that students of Mongolian, Chinese, and Japanese decent were prohibited from attending public schools with white children, once a separate school for these children had been created. The law was silent on African American children.[1] In 1893, the legislature further segregated education by race when it adopted an amendment adding Indian children to the list of students who must be excluded from public schools for white children once separate schools had been established. The only exception was for four-year-old kindergarten children. ("California segregation laws," 2004).

By 1918, all states had established public schools, most of which were segregated by race and gender. Black children in primary schools received a substantially inferior education to white children. Many southern states did not have public high schools for black students; black teacher's colleges took the place of secondary schools for a select few. According to Prof. Ronald L. F. Davis of California State University at Northridge,

> Many of the black colleges and normal schools serving African Americans were hardly colleges at all. Because no public high schools for black children existed in most of the southern states, the typical black teachers' college included curricula at the secondary level. As late as 1915, no public high schools for blacks existed in Mississippi, South Carolina, North Carolina, or Louisiana. Only one each existed in Florida, Delaware, and Maryland. Atlanta had none before the 1920s. Almost all southern blacks receiving a high school education prior to 1910 had graduated from private, usually church sponsored, schools.
>
> Those primary schools that did exist in the Jim Crow South offered substandard curricula, often in dilapidated and falling down shacks. Educator Booker T. Washington described them as "wretched little hovels with no light or warmth or comfort of any kind." Black teachers' salaries fell far below those paid white teachers, and many of the teachers were educated just at the primary level, especially in the rural areas. (Davis, n.d.)

By 1940, the quality of schools for African American children severely lagged the quality of schools for whites. According to researchers Tyack and Cuban, schools for African Americans "only received 12 percent of the revenues" as compared with schools for whites. The authors state that "Half of black teachers had gone no further than high school as compared with 7 percent of white teachers" and schools often lacked even the "most basic aids to learning—textbooks, slates and chalk, or desks" (Tyack &

[1]The California Supreme Court ruled in *Wysinger v. Crookshank,* 82 Cal. 588, January 29, 1890, that under California Political Code 1669, amended in 1880, African American children could not lawfully be excluded from white schools. Arthur Wysinger became the first African American student to be admitted to Visalia's high school.

Cuban, 1995, p. 23). In the South, school systems were designed to be a caste system that legally assigned African American children to unequal schools.

Prior to 1954, under the United States Constitution, it was legal to segregate African American children within the public schools. In 1954, the U.S. Supreme Court in *Brown v. Topeka Board of Education* ruled that "separate but equal schools" were unconstitutional. In 1955, in *Brown II*, the U.S. Supreme Court ordered that desegregation occur with "all deliberate speed." However, ten years after the 1954 Brown decision by the U.S. Supreme Court, "more than 99.5% of black students in the South, excluding Texas and Tennessee, still attend[ed] all-black schools" (Balkin & Rodriguez, n.d.).

By the 1960s and 1970s, there was finally a majority in the U.S. Congress to pass major laws that would significantly expand the civil rights for all citizens. During that time period, three laws were enacted that specifically expanded the rights of students, based on the belief that all students should be entitled to attend school without discrimination due to race, color, religion, national origin, or handicap. The three laws were:

• The Civil Rights Act (1964), which prohibited discrimination on the basis of race, color, sex, religion, or national origin. Title IV of the law (Desegregation of the Public Schools) authorized the government to sue on behalf of parents or students who were unable to bring suit for discrimination. In 1974, the Supreme Court in *Lau v. Nichols* interpreted "national origin" discrimination to include educational discrimination against English language learners, and required schools to provide educational programs to teach English to immigrant children. (Lau v. Nichols, 1974).

• Title IX (1972), which banned sex discrimination in schools that received federal funds. This new law radically changed women's sports, which previously received far fewer funds than men's sports. The new law required schools and colleges, which received federal funds, to offer equal opportunities based on sex.

• The Education for All Handicapped Children Act (1975), now known as the Individuals with Disabilities Act (IDEA), which assured that all children with disabilities had available to them a free and appropriate public education, and which emphasized special education and related services designed to meet their unique needs.

It is well known that IDEA now ensures free and appropriate education to all children with special needs. What is often not known is that the law was a civil rights response for two groups of children: more than one million children with disabilities who had limited access to free and appropriate education within the public schools, and one million other children with disabilities who were excluded entirely from the public education system (U. S. Office of Special Education Programs, 2007).

These three laws significantly expanded the rights of women, minorities, and the disabled to receive an education. However, even with the passage of laws that opened the doors for many students, significant achievement gaps persisted, and still exist today for special education students, low-income students, and for many racial minorities:

> Although more than three-quarters of white and Asian students in the United States earn diplomas, high school outcomes are much worse for others. Among Latinos, 56 percent successfully finish high school, while 54 percent of African-Americans and 51 percent of Native Americans graduate. (Swanson, 2010)

One way to measure this achievement gap for low-income and minority students is by measuring high school graduation rates. The following chart breaks down high school graduation rates by race. As of the 2007–2008 school year, Black, Hispanic, and American Indian/Alaska Native children lag behind white and Asian children in high school graduation rates.

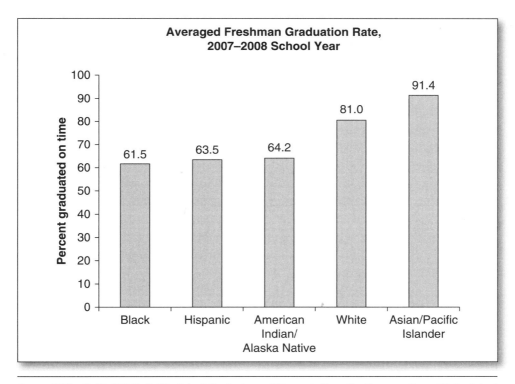

Source: Stillwell, R. (2010). *Public School Graduates and Dropouts From the Common Core of Data: School Year 2007–08* (NCES 2010-341). National Center for Education Statistics, Institute of Education Sciences, U.S. Department of Education. Washington, DC. Retrieved from http://nces.ed.gov/pubsearch/pubsinfo .asp?pubid=2010341.

Over the last 200 years, as the states and the federal government have played an increased role in education, many minority students have still been left behind. Legal obstacles are only some of the many barriers to education access; other factors, such as where children live, poverty, parental education level, and the beliefs that teachers and policymakers hold, also affect a child's access to a quality education. While changing laws is often a long and difficult process, community and educator beliefs may be even harder to change than the laws, and may persist even when the laws have been changed. Racial prejudice, wrote Chief Justice Lemuel Shaw in *Roberts v. The City of Boston* in 1850, "is not created by law, and probably cannot be changed by law" (Massachusetts Foundation for the Humanities, 2005, May 17). At least, it cannot be changed by law alone.

LIMITATION TWO: CHANGING MINDSETS AND LIMITING BELIEFS ABOUT LEARNING

While legislatures can repeal and courts can strike down laws that discriminate against some citizens, legislatures and courts cannot change what citizens believe and how all people behave. Despite the 1954 Supreme Court's ruling in *Brown v. Topeka Board of Education,* few school districts desegregated voluntarily. For example, in 1957, Arkansas Governor Orval Faubus posted members of the National Guard at Central High School in Little Rock to prevent the court-ordered admission of black students. When President Eisenhower intervened to enforce desegregation, Governor Faubus eventually closed all four high schools in Little Rock. In 1959, the Prince Edward County, Virginia, school system chose to close all of its public schools rather than desegregate them. And in 1963, at his inauguration as Governor of Alabama, George Wallace proclaimed, "In the name of the greatest people that have ever trod this earth, I draw the line in the dust and toss the gauntlet before the feet of tyranny . . . and I say . . . Segregation now! Segregation tomorrow! Segregation forever!" (Balkin & Rodriguez, n.d.).

Even today, after the passage of many state and federal civil rights laws, many urban schools in the United States are still racially segregated. While legislation and court rulings are necessary, they are insufficient to entirely change mindsets, beliefs, and private behavior. In this section, we will discuss how an educator's values and beliefs can also have a powerful impact on a child's access to quality education.

While the civil rights laws of the 1960s and 1970s are admirable and necessary, and are enforceable by law, the government cannot change a teacher's beliefs about a child's ability to learn and the teacher's learning expectations. Therefore, unless schools are also able to create a school climate that expects all teachers to teach all students at high levels and create conditions for teachers to believe that high achievement for all students is possible, more laws and regulations won't be sufficient. A teacher's low expectations for students, based on a belief that certain students cannot learn, or learn as well, has a similar adverse impact on disadvantaged students as actual school rules and laws that separate students by socioeconomic class, gender, or race.

From our observations, the response of teachers to unsuccessful learning in their students often flows from the teacher's views on intelligence. Too often, teachers attribute student failure to a lack of "natural" ability, or they blame failure on the lack of parental support. In contrast, educators who hold more liberating views about intelligence, or Carol Dweck's "growth mindset," will seek out different pedagogical approaches.

> In a growth mindset, people believe that their most basic abilities can be developed through dedication and hard work—brains and talent are just the starting point. This view creates a love of learning and a resilience that is essential for great accomplishment. Virtually all great people have had these qualities. (Dweck, 2011)

A powerful example of how beliefs can affect achievement is found in the changes that have taken place over the past four decades in women's sports. Watching the 2008 U.S. women's basketball team win the gold medal in Beijing brought back memories of when Americans used to believe that women could not play sports as well as men. Prior to the Title IX rule changes that were implemented in 1972, a women's basketball team consisted of six players, not five. Players were only allowed to dribble twice before passing and only certain players, called rovers, were allowed to cross the half court line and run the full length of the court.

Why did these different rules for female athletes exist? Why were our beliefs limited in regard to athletics and women's capacities? Anyone old enough to remember watching women play this diluted game of basketball might also remember that these rules reinforced prevailing beliefs about women's inability to be athletic and competitive. With Title IX and a shift in cultural norms, the prevailing assumptions about women athletes began to change. Title IX forced schools to provide women with access to a much wider range of athletic opportunities, skillful coaching with high expectations, and improved practice conditions. Changes in the law and a change in beliefs have both made it possible for more women athletes to perform at much higher levels.

What beliefs might be limiting the development of students today? Could we possibly see, for example, a change in mathematics achievement if we explored and changed our perceptions about who can do math? There seems to be a belief that when it comes to mathematics, "some people have it, while others don't." Would our schools, our curricula, and our grouping patterns look different if we believed that the overwhelming majority of our students have the capacity to think mathematically?

We have listed below a set of limiting beliefs that exist in many schools today and contrast them to more liberating assumptions that have the potential of affecting how students achieve (adapted from Saphier & D'Auria, 1993).

LIMITING BELIEFS ABOUT INTELLIGENCE

- Intelligence is fixed. Only the few bright children can achieve at a high level.
- Speed is what counts. Faster is smarter.
- Inborn intelligence is the determinant of success.
- Mistakes are a sign of weakness.
- Smart students work independently.

LIBERATING BELIEFS ABOUT INTELLIGENCE

- Intelligence is malleable. All children are capable of high achievement, not just the fastest and most confident.
- It's OK not to understand everything the first time around.
- Consistent effort is the main determinant of success.
- Mistakes help one learn.
- Smart students seek out assistance, resources, and alternative pathways.

In this section, we discussed the role that beliefs and mindsets, both conscious and subconscious, play in creating barriers to education at high levels for all students. The beliefs of educators about who is entitled to an education and who is capable of learning at high levels have a real impact on the outcome for students. In the next section, we will explore how school leaders in the early 20th century believed that schools must be highly standardized in order to be efficient and cost effective. Their goal was to ensure that only some students were educated at high levels.

This third limitation, overly standardized schools, is still a major obstacle limiting a school or a school district's capacity to educate all students at high levels.

LIMITATION THREE: STANDARDIZATION VERSUS DIFFERENTIATION

In 2008, Harvard Business School Professor Clayton Christensen and his coauthors harshly criticized the level of standardization in American schools. They wrote,

> In summary, the current educational system—the way it trains teachers, the way it groups students, the way the curriculum is designed, and the way school buildings are laid out—is designed for standardization. If the United States is serious about leaving no child behind, it cannot teach its students with standardized methods. Today's system was designed at a time when standardization was seen as a virtue. It is an intricately interdependent system. Only an administrator suffering from virulent masochism would attempt to teach each student in the way his or her brain is wired to learn within this monolithic batch system. Schools need a new system. (Christensen, Horn, & Johnson, 2008, pp. 37–38)

Standardization in American schools has its roots in our educational history. A brief examination of the history of standardization in American schools will elucidate how belief in scientific management and the application of the "factory model" to education led to the creation of schools that were not designed for all students. In this section, we examine the fundamental belief systems that led to standardization, the origins of these beliefs, their impact on student performance, and the limitations the standardization model has placed on teacher collaboration.

America's schools were never designed to educate all students at high levels. Around the time of the American Revolution, cities and towns began establishing one-room schoolhouses as the institutional means to foster democracy and a moral society. From 1770 to 1890, one-room schoolhouses were the prevailing model of American education. Individual teachers were hired by local boards of selectmen to teach elementary students the academic basics. In 1890, only 5% of students graduated from high school.

By the late 1800s, curriculum was standardized through reliance on textbooks. These textbooks served as a "crutch" for teachers who had little knowledge and expertise in the areas they were expected to teach. As late as 1918, "more than half of America's elementary-school teachers had two or less years of academic and professional training beyond high school. In this context, textbooks functioned as undeniable crutches" (Clifford, 1978, p. 158) to support teachers and standardize education. This reliance on textbooks to guide instruction still exists today in many classrooms. For example, as late as 2005, 20 U.S. states still decided at the state board level which textbooks could be used by local school districts (Zinth, 2005). Since these states included Texas, Florida, and California, three of the largest states in the country, textbook publishers have little choice but to follow the curriculum standards mandated by these large states, effectively standardizing textbooks for all states.

By the early 1900s, economic circumstances and significant increases in immigration made it necessary to educate large numbers of students. Standardization increased as the predominant education model shifted from one-room schoolhouses to multiunit schools. In these new multiunit schools, the number of pupils per classroom was based not on the needs of students, but on fixed student-to-teacher ratios. The student day was organized not around how much time each student needed to learn the curriculum, but on a fixed number of minutes per class. Students were taught by age group, regardless of their proficiency in the curriculum. This multiunit school was based on the "factory" model, and these schools were actually run like factories: ringing bells, specialized subjects, and children taught in batches (age group or "date of manufacture"). This standardized, factory-based, multiunit school model was designed to run efficiently and sort students—it was never designed or intended to help all students achieve at high levels.

Additionally, teacher collaboration did not increase with the move from one-room schoolhouses to multiunit schools. According to professor emeritus Dan Lortie at the University of Chicago, "Teachers' work . . . was not radically altered by the development of the multi-unit school. . . . Schools were organized around teacher separation rather than teacher interdependence" (Lortie, 2002, p. 14). In the multiunit school, teachers still functioned independently of one another in their instruction; in some ways, these new schools effectively functioned as one-room schoolhouses under one roof.

The famous educator Edward Thorndike, also the former president of the American Psychological Association, believed that "creating a better, more predictable world" was the goal of education. Thorndike "strived to develop a science of learning so that brick by brick a science of education could be built" (Eisner, 1983, p. 6). Thorndike's "better and more predictable world" guided by a science of education, was not, however, the world we strive for today, in which all children have equal access to education. Thorndike's "science" of education was framed by his explicit racial and ethnic bias, and by white supremacy and the principles of Social Darwinism. He did not believe that Jewish and African American children had the same capacity to learn as Anglo-American white children, and in 1912, he stated that it would be "wasteful" to educate them (p. 41).

Thorndike advocated that teachers control and test children, since a child was an "empty organism" whom teachers had to fill (Getzels, 1978, p. 489). Teachers controlled students in classrooms, with the teacher in the front of the classroom and students sitting in chairs bolted to the floor facing the teacher. Students did not collaborate. Testing was a large part of Thorndike's repertoire (Clifford, 1978, p. 114).

In these schools, not only were the students highly controlled, so were the teachers. Elliot Eisner, former Professor of Education at Stanford, wrote that the role of teachers in 1910 was highly regulated. He said that "Teachers were regarded as workers to be supervised by specialists who made sure that goals were being attained, that teachers were performing as prescribed, and that the public who paid for the schools were getting their money's worth . . . The task was to get teachers to follow one best method, a method that scientific management of education would prescribe" (Eisner, 1983, p. 7). Scientific management has been defined as "the administration of a business or industry based on experimental studies of efficiency; the application of the principles of the scientific method to managing a business or industry" ("Scientific management," 2012).

According to Lortie, even in the 1920s and 1930s, "[School officials] saw teachers as similar to factory hands—as agents charged with implementing detailed specifications developed in central headquarters" (Lortie, p. 5). By 1925, "Thirty-four state departments of education managed to 'standardize' more than 40,000 schools" (Tyack & Cuban, 1995, p. 20). During this time period, school officials continued to import "scientific management" from business, since they believed that scientific management was the best way to achieve educational efficiency in schools.

In 1959, James Conant, former president of Harvard University, further standardized education by introducing the use of standardized aptitude tests for undergraduate admission. He also proposed that graduating classes have at least 100 students in order to be effective, and that the day would have seven or eight periods of approximately 45 minutes each (Conant, 1959, pp. 64–65).

The next major historical stage in the standardization of schools came from new federal court decisions and laws. Until *Brown v. Board of Education* in 1954, the federal government had almost no role in education. States were largely responsible for setting educational policy, funding schools, establishing curriculum standards, and licensing teachers. In 1979, Congress created the U.S. Department of Education. In 2001, Congress passed a change to the Elementary and Secondary Education Act, commonly known as No Child Left Behind (NCLB). NCLB was the first national law that mandated educational standards for all 50 states, annual testing of students, and accountability standards. NCLB included enforcement provisions under which schools would be sanctioned for not making annual yearly progress toward rigid, objectively defined academic standards.

At the state level, laws were enacted to protect workers' rights, ensure quality teaching, and improve educational quality. Such laws granted workers in numerous states the right to collectively bargain for contracts, increased licensure requirements for teachers, mandated teaching evaluation processes and standards, and mandated the curriculum that must be taught in schools.

Although in the 1950s and 1960s there was an increased move towards greater equality in education, the belief systems that underlie the fundamental structure of schooling did not change. According to Jeannie Oakes, an expert on educational equity at the University of California (Los Angeles), the most remarkable thing about the mid-20th century was not the move toward greater educational equality, but the intransigence of the essential structural properties of schooling even in the face of social and legal reform (Oakes, 1986). Although new funding was provided to a wide array of initiatives aimed at closing the achievement gap for poor and minority students, such as Head Start and Title I, this

> generous funding was given to programs that did not upset (a) the control of education, (b) the content or organization of schooling, (c) the pattern or distribution of educational resources, or (d) eventual social or economic payoff for differing educational credentials. For most people in decision-making positions, the only acceptable means of "equalizing" educational opportunities was to allocate additional resources to overcome deficits—to change individual students rather than to change the conduct of schooling or to examine its underlying assumptions. (p. 67)

According to Oakes, by the 1980s, approximately 30 years after *Brown v. Topeka Board of Education*, differentiated schooling and tracking had not changed in the vast majority of schools, and the role of these structures in perpetuating the achievement gap between middle-class white students and poor and minority students remained unquestioned and unchallenged; any gaps that existed were still justified in terms of individual and cultural differences. Although laws and funding formulas had changed, the myth persisted that American schools provided an equal, democratic opportunity to all.

While Oakes wrote this article in the 1980s, the situation remains largely the same today. Though some of the rationales for standardization have changed since they were first introduced, the basic structure of schools has not, and the tendency to rationalize away the achievement gaps through individuals and cultural difference—the belief that some children simply cannot learn—remains in effect today as strongly as ever.

Though Social Darwinism is no longer the philosophy of prominent educational leaders (such as Thorndike), this model is still widely used today, and when poor and minority children fail, the contribution of the system itself to that failure is rarely challenged. According to Oakes, "The failure of disadvantaged children (especially if they have received 'remediative' or 'compensatory' services) becomes a matter of their own deficiencies—social, economic, educational or linguistic—and not of the schools' inadequate response to them. " (p. 72)

More standardization, with higher stakes, must be the answer, according to proponents of NCLB. The problem lies not with the structure of schools, but with the lack of rigid standards and "one-size-fits-all" curricula, and measurement of student achievement by standardized tests. But this "standardization" of education is not culturally neutral, and students tracked into different groups still receive a different quality of education; as Oakes puts it, "There is no presumption that high status knowledge is appropriate for all." (p. 74)

As early as 1920, "test-score based student segregation and academic tracking" dominated the Detroit Public Schools (Levin, 1991, p. 73). Today, standardized tests have become even more common, and are used to track students in a wide variety of ways, beginning in grade school. These standardized tests act to "commodify" education, measuring "worker productivity" as in the factory, quantifying learning, and acting as "quality controls" on the educational system. Again we hear echoes of scientific management. According to Oakes, "a disturbing result is that quantitative determinations of quality have a disproportionately negative effect on poor and minority children" (p. 74).

African American children, for example, are disproportionately tracked into special education based in part on local and state standardized tests. A 1998 study by the U.S. Department of Education found that "black students were nearly three times as likely as white students to be labeled mentally retarded" (Losen & Orfield, 2002, pp. 22–23). The overrepresentation of African American and Hispanic students in special education was further verified by Mathew Deninger, policy analyst for the Massachusetts Department of Elementary and Secondary Education, who said,

> African American students were approximately 1.3 times (approximately 30 percent) more likely than non-African American students to be found eligible for special education. Similarly, Hispanic students were 1.2 times (approximately 21 percent) more likely than non-Hispanic students to be found eligible for special education. (2008, p. 4)

Recently, there has been a growing backlash against rigid standardization and an increasing belief that we are overregulating and overstandardizing schools. There is also recognition that raising standards without increasing the funding to meet these standards will not be successful. For example, while the National Education Association (NEA) supports the goals of NCLB, the NEA has been a staunch critic of the law, "maintaining that it is an unfunded mandate with unattainable student-achievement goals" (Hoff, 2007). Recently, Carmel Martin, the Assistant Secretary for Planning, Evaluation, and Policy Development at the U.S. Department of Education, stated,

> Under current law, it's a one-size-fits-all intervention that we don't think [is] moving the dime for these students. We think that by allowing states and districts greater flexibility in figuring how to tackle areas of weakness, they're going to have a better shot at overcoming challenges for students in historically overlooked subgroups. (Klein, 2011)

The deep historical roots of standardization influence our current way of doing business in school. While we need to maintain and expand access to a quality education for all students, we are not going to be able to achieve it with a one-size-fits-all model. Many scholars and ordinary citizens today are speaking out against the overstandardization of schools by states and the federal government. For example, Ronald Wolk, former editor of *Education Week*, said,

> Standardization and uniformity may work with cars and computers, but it doesn't work with humans. Today's student body is the most diverse in history. An education system that treats all students alike denies that reality. (2009, p. 30)
>
> The issue is not whether standards are necessary. Schools without standards are unacceptable. Society should indeed hold high expectations for all students, but those expectations should reflect

the values of the family and society—doing one's best, obeying the rules, and mutual respect—and not simply the archaic academic demands of college-admissions offices. We should be preparing young people for life, not just for college. (p. 36)

In the next section, we will discuss the fourth limitation to highly effective schools for all learners—teacher isolation, a product of overstandardization that significantly limits the capacity of teachers to learn from colleagues and to collectively improve learning for all students.

LIMITATION FOUR: TEACHER ISOLATION VERSUS TEACHER COLLABORATION, LEADERSHIP, AND ENGAGEMENT

Throughout the history of U.S. schools, the vast majority of teachers have spent their workday isolated from their colleagues. In a study by Robert Rothberg, 80% of teachers agreed with a description of their classroom as "a private world which no one besides you and your students entered" (1986, p. 320). Kenneth Tye reported that "teachers tend to be isolated in their own classrooms, in control of what goes on there, and satisfied with the situation as it is" (Tye, 1981, p. 52). Only in the past few years have school systems begun to break down the walls of teacher isolation by establishing common planning time for teachers who share the same work. One such example of teacher collaboration is the professional learning communities.

When teachers are able to collaborate with one another, share leadership, and engage with each other, the collective capacity to improve learning for all students is increased. In the paragraphs that follow, we explore the historical roots that contributed to teacher isolation in schools.

As already discussed, until the early 1900s, most teachers in America taught in one-room schoolhouses. In such settings, teachers were the only instructors and could not collaborate with other educators on lessons and curriculum design. The rapid increase in school enrollments and construction of multiunit schools in the early 1900s did little to reduce teacher isolation. According to Professor Dan C. Lortie, "Teachers' work, in short, was not radically altered by the development of the multi-unit school. . . . As before, the teacher continued to work largely alone" (Lortie, p. 14).

Lortie identifies isolation as a product of institutional characteristics firmly grounded in the historical development of schools: namely, the growth of the multiunit school from the one-room schoolhouse and high teacher turnover rates due in part to the ban on married female schoolteachers (p. 14). Although the ban on married female schoolteachers was lifted in the 1940s, the patterns of teacher isolation that Lortie describes in his book, *Schoolteacher*, nonetheless remain largely true today.

Lortie describes the "egg-crate" architecture of school buildings and school cultures that together physically separate teachers from each other by classroom and also professionally separate them by grade and by subject. Schools, Lortie argues, were organized based on teacher independence rather than teacher interdependence. Even today, teachers are assigned a group of students for the whole day in elementary schools and for a class period in the upper grades; and they spend most of their day teaching those students within their four walls, with little time to interact with other teachers.

Lortie also describes how in the past very high rates of teacher turnover made it impossible for teachers to work interdependently in any sustainable way. Teachers had restricted opportunities for feedback from colleagues, rarely had opportunities to visit other teachers' classrooms, and were evaluated by supervisors only a few times per year (Lortie, pp. 69–73). Even though some of the causes for high teacher turnover are different today than they were in the first half of the twentieth century, high rates of teacher turnover in some school systems continue to be an obstacle to creating a culture of teacher interdependence and collaboration.

In the early 1980s, teacher isolation was further documented in a study of 1,350 elementary and secondary school teachers. Educational researcher John Goodlad found that isolation is a widespread characteristic of professional life in schools. He wrote, "Approximately three quarters of our [teacher] samples at all levels of schooling indicated that they would like to observe other teachers at work" (Goodlad, 1983, p. 188). In a 2009 study titled *The American Teacher*, 67% of teachers and 78% of principals reported that greater collaboration among teachers and school leaders would have a major impact on improving student achievement (MetLife, 2009, p. 9).

Unfortunately, the culture of most schools makes it difficult for young teachers to crack the walls of privatism (Hargreaves & Fullan, 1992, p. 292). According to the 2009 MetLife study, teachers spend only 2.7 hours per week, on average, in structured collaboration with other teachers and leaders (MetLife, 2009, p. 15). Isolated teachers have very little time outside their classrooms to collaborate with other teachers to mutually develop curriculum and common lessons and to share effective practices.

Studies of effective schools show that in them teachers are far less likely to work in isolation. One such study conducted by Susan J. Rosenholtz found that these schools, rather than being isolated work settings, "are usually

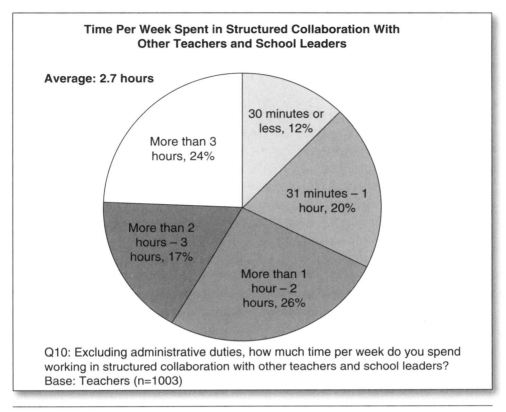

Time Per Week Spent in Structured Collaboration With Other Teachers and School Leaders

Average: 2.7 hours

- 30 minutes or less, 12%
- 31 minutes – 1 hour, 20%
- More than 1 hour – 2 hours, 26%
- More than 2 hours – 3 hours, 17%
- More than 3 hours, 24%

Q10: Excluding administrative duties, how much time per week do you spend working in structured collaboration with other teachers and school leaders? Base: Teachers (n=1003)

Source: Metlife, 2009.

places of intellectual sharing, collaborative planning, and collegial work" (Rosenholtz, 1985, p. 365). Researcher Judith Warren Little also found that successful schools are distinguished by norms of collegiality among staff. In a research study involving six urban desegregated schools, she wrote

> In successful schools, more than unsuccessful ones, teachers valued and participated in norms of collegiality and continuous improvement (experimentation); they pursued a greater range of professional interactions with fellow teachers or administrators, including talk about instruction, structured observation, and shared planning or preparation. They did so with greater frequency, with a greater precise shared language. (1982, p. 325)

In the next section, we describe the impact of inadequate teacher and administrator professional development on student learning. Following that, we discuss the gap that often exists between teaching and student learning, and how, when these activities are independent, a teacher's capacity to teach all students effectively is much more limited.

LIMITATION FIVE: A NARROW VIEW OF PROFESSIONAL DEVELOPMENT

While we are confident that the vast majority of school districts hire the very best teachers available, we are also confident that educators need high-quality professional development[2] for the remainder of their careers. Unfortunately, the majority of teachers in the United States do not engage in professional development that is likely to improve teaching practice (Steiner, 2004, p. 1). In this section, we examine how a school district's narrow view of professional development limits teacher capacity to provide high quality teaching and learning.

Professional development is a relatively new concept in American education. In 1970, the National Staff Development Council (NSDC) was formed at a conference in Racine, Wisconsin. There were only 17 people in attendance. It wasn't until 1980 that the NSDC formed as a legal entity and issued its first semiannual *Journal of Staff Development*.

During most of the 20th century, school districts offered very little professional development. According to Lortie, professional development "tended to be measured in days, and even hours, rather than weeks or months. . . . Provisions for additional training within school systems [were] sparse" (1975, p. 60). A 2000 study conducted for the National Center for Education Statistics found that teachers spent about a day or less in professional development on any one content area per year (National Center for Education Statistics, 2000, p. 70).

In schools today, the two most common forms of professional development are short-term in-service days that are designed to teach specific ideas, techniques, or materials; and university-based courses that focus on content and not application (Steiner, 2004, p. 3). Unfortunately, research shows that these two approaches do not lead to substantive and lasting changes in teaching that has a significant effect on student learning (Cohen & Hill, 2001; Parsad, Lewis, & Farris, 2001; Porter et al., 2000). In a study of mathematics and science teachers, M. S. Garet, who was a chief research scientist for the American Institutes for Research, and others studied 1,027 teachers to determine what makes professional development effective (Garet et al., 2001). His research team found that short-term workshops outside the school day had little impact on teaching (p. 920).

---

[2]Learning Forward defines professional development as "a comprehensive, sustained, and intensive approach to improving teachers' and principals' effectiveness in raising student achievement" (Retrieved from http://www.learningforward.org/standfor/definition .cfm#DefinitionRources).

Professional development has been shown to be more effective when provided over a sustained period of time and when there is time for teachers to discuss and reflect on what they have learned. A 1999 study by the U.S. Department of Education found that when teachers report their professional development activities extended over a longer period of time, they cite improvements in teaching practice (Steiner, 2004, p. 3).

A 2005 study conducted by the Australian government examined the links between teacher professional development and student learning outcomes. The study concluded that student learning increases when professional development has a "strong content focus, as well as an emphasis on other features such as follow-up, active learning, feedback and professional community" (Meiers & Ingvarson, 2005, p. 84).

These studies strongly suggest that in order for a school system to more effectively implement professional development, it must shift from short-term professional development programs to longer-term programs and from university-based courses selected by individual teachers to district-sponsored programs selected by both teachers and administrators. Shifting to longer-term professional development programs provides teachers with deeper learning experiences and more time to apply their new knowledge. To make this change requires lengthening professional development programs from the commonly used one-day workshop to programs that are "presented in an intensive, sustained, and continuous manner over time" (Wei et al., 2009). According to a study of 1,300 studies on the effectiveness of professional development,

> Studies that had more than 14 hours of professional development showed a positive and significant effect on student achievement for professional development. The three studies that involved the least amount of professional development (5–14 hours total) showed no statistically significant effects on student achievement. (Yoon et al., 2007, p. iv)

The report goes on to state that "an average of 49 hours in nine studies—can boost their students' achievement by about 21 points" (p. iii).

In order to ensure that teachers are engaged in high quality, long-term professional development and that programs are tied to district goals, we recommend that districts establish districtwide professional development committees. It is our experience that when teachers and administrators collaborate to design a district's professional development program, the result is much more comprehensive and more likely to meet student needs. When individual teachers design their own university-based professional development programs, they may take courses of personal interest to them; on the other hand, when numerous teachers are engaged in district-sponsored programs together, they are more likely to collaborate on district goals and transfer the knowledge and skills they learned to the classroom.

Research shows that the most effective professional development takes place every day for every educator. The goal is to create a web of active adult learners who are connected to each other within a school and to educators throughout the world. This newer approach to professional development includes: lesson study groups, teacher data teams, action research projects, mentoring programs, case study discussions, coaching, district-sponsored courses, programs offered by professional organizations, and technology-based distance learning. All of these approaches require educators to study their professional practices as a team and to receive specific feedback from colleagues. All of these group approaches take place over weeks and months and allow teachers to both share information and push each other to improve practice.

We have no doubt that today's hardworking teachers come to school each day and do the best job they know how to do. However, given our goal that all students achieve at high levels, it is unrealistic to expect that teachers will succeed with all students unless they also have a robust, continuous professional development program targeted to student needs. Most importantly, we see professional development as something that needs to occur every day in schools. Significant adult learning occurs when teachers analyze student work, collaborate with one another, and adjust instruction to better meet the needs of students. Every day, learning must occur not only for the students, but for the adults as well.

In the final section of this chapter, we discuss what happens when teaching and learning are an interactive process rather than separate acts. We will discuss how teachers who seek feedback from multiple sources are better able to modify their instruction in real time and to teach more students effectively.

LIMITATION SIX: TEACHING AND STUDENT LEARNING AS SEPARATE ACTS VERSUS TEACHING AND LEARNING AS AN INTERACTIVE PROCESS

For most of our educational history, teaching has been the central domain of teachers and learning the main activity of students. In many ways, the teaching and learning process has been segregated by roles and responsibilities. While this separation may appear eminently logical to some, separating the teaching process from the student learning process significantly limits a teacher's ability to modify lessons in real time based on student needs. In addition, if a teacher's instruction is also cut off from feedback from colleagues, his or her capacity to improve instruction is diminished.

In order to unleash the potential of all educators within our schools and maximize their capacity to educate all students, it is vital that all teachers continuously learn from their students, supervisors, and colleagues in order to expand their knowledge and skills. As a teacher moves from an isolated teaching world to a collaborative learning community, he or she will need to increasingly seek and share feedback in three ways:

1. Between teacher and students;

2. Between teacher and supervisor; and

3. Between teacher and colleagues.

The interactive and dynamic process is represented in the diagram that follows.

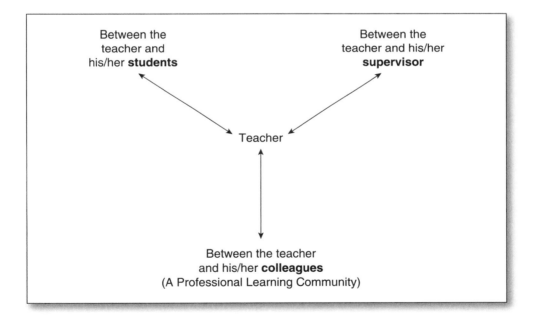

The sharing of information between a teacher and students is the first component of an interactive teacher-student learning process. In order to shift from a batch model of education to a more individualized approach, teachers will need feedback from their students as they teach their lessons. By gathering information from students while a lesson is being taught, a teacher is able to adjust the lesson based on actual student needs at the time. This continuous two-way feedback process should increase the level of student learning and student engagement. Some of the ways teachers can gather information about student learning in real time include teacher questions, student questions, teacher observations, student work products, and the use of formative assessments.

The ongoing dialogue between a teacher and supervisor is a second component of an interactive learning process; in this dialogue, teachers can receive feedback about their work and how their efforts stack up against standards and student results. When supervisor feedback is closely connected to the ongoing teaching-learning process, there is a greater likelihood that student achievement will increase. In too many systems, we have observed supervision and evaluation processes that provide little to no useful feedback to educators.

The establishment of a professional learning community (PLC) between and among teachers is the third way teachers can learn from each other and improve classroom instruction. In a PLC, teachers who share grades or subject areas meet during common planning periods to discuss student progress as measured against curriculum standards and to develop future lessons and intervention strategies. The shift from teacher isolation to an interdependent team allows the classroom teacher to gain the insights of colleagues and thus to increase teaching effectiveness.

In some school systems, we have observed that teachers insist that they have taught (or covered) the material adequately and that any lack of learning must be the student's fault. These teachers, dividing teaching and learning into separate acts, limit their capacity to learn what their students know day-to-day and to change their instruction based on that knowledge. Separating teaching from learning ensures that achievement gaps will remain static or even increase. When teachers gather information from students, supervisors, and colleagues, they are more able to nimbly respond to student needs on a continuous basis in real time.

WHERE DO WE GO FROM HERE?

For hundreds of years, we, as Americans, never attempted to educate all students at high levels. American schools were designed based on the goals and values of many prior generations, which we do not always share. The national goal of educating all students to proficient levels only became federal law in 2001 with the passage of No Child Left Behind (NCLB). While some people criticize the means and resources of the 2001 law, the goal of high academic achievement for all students was a huge change in American policy.

NCLB created a framework to establish academic standards and mandated annual student testing with sanctions if academic standards were not achieved. The law did not, however, do anything to change the structure of schools themselves or the quality of teaching in schools.

Where do we go from here? The first step is recognizing that schools were designed in a different era and for different goals. The second step is starting a dialogue on how to restructure schools in ways that will foster the potential of millions of educators to educate all students at high levels.

In Chapter 1, we have described six historical factors that have limited the capacity of school systems to educate all students at high levels. The good news is that these limitations did not come down from Mount Sinai. These institutional and psychological obstacles can be overcome. In the remaining sections of the book, we describe how the limitations of the past can be eliminated or reduced and how we can unleash the collective intellectual power of educators to innovate and to more effectively educate all students.

In Chapters 2 through 6, we describe four conditions that are necessary to overcome the limitations of the past and to energize all educators, working as a team, to innovate, share best practices, and find effective and pragmatic ways to educate all students. In Chapter 7, once a school has created a culture of innovation, we will examine numerous ways interest groups can stop a culture of change. Finally, in Chapter 8, we discuss how school leaders can overcome opposition to changes needed to improve learning and how they can diffuse innovations throughout their schools and their school system.

2 The Four Right Drivers of Change

It was about 2:30 p.m. on a beautiful Friday afternoon in San Francisco when one of us (Paul Ash) had the opportunity to speak with a very well-known educational writer and researcher who was selling his new educational program at a national conference (his name is withheld to avoid any unintentional embarrassment):

Later that afternoon, I entered a small conference room at a nearby hotel. After refreshments, the author and I, along with a handful of other people, sat down at a conference table to discuss the author's new program.

After some discussion about the new program, I started asking questions and soon was engaged in a one-to-one conversation. Not wanting to dominate the meeting, I asked the other attendees if they would like to make comments or to ask questions. I was shocked when all four of them declined and told me they worked for him or were other vendors. I was the only real potential client! To my surprise, he didn't end the meeting after thirty minutes, and we continued talking.

I finally gained the courage to ask the question that had been bothering me for years. I asked, "You and other researchers have written numerous books on what educators should do to improve schools. How do administrators put all of these ideas together to create a K–12 plan that works for all children?" To my surprise, he said, "How the hell do I know?" Knowing that this answer was not helpful, he then said to pick one idea from a respected researcher and deeply focus on implementing the one idea well. That was the sum of his advice.

I walked out of this meeting after an hour and a half stunned that such an expert was not able to recommend how to apply his research insights to create a specific set of action steps for a whole school or a whole school system.

While we are sure that implementing one program very well would positively improve education for some students within a school or school system, one new initiative, no matter how well implemented, could not be sufficient. We also know, based on the research conducted by Douglas Reeves and others, that launching a wide array of new K–12 gap-closing initiatives will eventually lead to ineffective implementation due to initiative fatigue.

INITIATIVE FATIGUE

In Chapter 1, we described six historical factors that limit a school system's capacity to raise academic achievement. Initiative fatigue is one more factor that limits a school system's capacity to improve beyond its resources. Reeves, in his book *Transforming Development Into Student Results,* describes the Law of Initiative Fatigue and its high impact on professional learning:

> Education leaders have three essential resources: time, money, and emotional energy. Time is fixed. Financial resources are typically fixed and, in the present economy, diminishing. Emotional energy is variable but has limits that are exhausted quickly by school leaders who ignore the reality that even the most dedicated employee can be resilient but will refuse to be an eternal Bobo doll, rising from each punch to endure another blow. The Law of Initiative Fatigue states that when the number of initiatives increases while time, resources, and emotional energy are constant, then each new initiative—no matter how well conceived or well intentioned—will receive fewer minutes, dollars, and ounces of emotional energy than its predecessors. (2010, p. 26)

As practitioners, we have all experienced the impact of initiative fatigue. In our efforts to improve teaching and learning, year after year, we add new initiatives at a greater rate than that of the number of initiatives we remove. Not only does this practice lead to exhausted teachers, the practice also leads to poor results due to insufficient resources, support, and time for each new initiative.

In no way do we intend to blame administrators for generating more and more initiatives each year to solve major problems. We know the intent is good. The problem is that increasing the number of initiatives generally does not produce significant results and it is not sustainable. We also know that focusing on only one initiative will have very limited impact on students. On the other hand, focusing on many initiatives does not work due to initiative fatigue. Did Goldilocks have the right answer— selecting "just the right" number of initiatives? Based on our experience, significant increases in student academic and behavioral success are not a function of the number of well-intentioned initiatives. If that were the case, then many hard-working, well-functioning school systems in the United States would have already closed the achievement gap for special education students, students of color, English language learners, and low-income students.

In Chapter 1, we suggested that the vast majority of U.S. school systems have reached the limits of their capacity, which explains why they have not been able to provide all students with the education they need. At the start of the present chapter, we discussed why adding one initiative after another is not the answer for all students on a systemwide basis. In the remaining sections of Chapter 2, we propose a systemwide approach to increasing educator capacity that will lead to increased learning for all students.

CREATING A K–12 LEARNING SCHOOL SYSTEM FOR ALL EDUCATORS

For those readers who may be skeptical, we ask that you consider the following questions: Have researchers ever shown that teacher isolation is a more educationally effective strategy than teachers collaborating toward common goals? Is there evidence that top-down management is more effective than teacher problem-solving and leadership at all levels of the school system? Is there evidence that school structures based on standardization are more effective than school structures that are differentiated based on actual student needs? Lastly, is there any evidence in the private or public sector that employees do not need frequent training and quality supervision throughout their careers? The answer to each question is "No." There is no research that supports the claim that high employee performance is based on isolation, top-down management, standardization, and lack of employee training. These strategies of the past have limited the capacity of teachers and administrators.

The educational needs of students are highly complex and constantly changing, which means that educators must constantly challenge themselves to learn new ways to reach students. When school districts create K–12 learning school systems for all educators, based on the principles of collaboration, multiple levels of decision making, differentiated practices, and professional development, the overall quality of educational practice

The Importance of Trust

- Embracing leadership that supports and serves the needs of teachers and students
- Communicating openly and honestly
- Engaging in difficult conversations
- Seeing conflict as a means to gain deep commitment to common goals
- Building a culture that supports the learning of both students and educators
- Honoring group norms

Collaboration in All Directions—Elevating the Importance of Teamwork

- Understanding that none of us is as smart as all of us
- Utilizing teamwork as a central lever of reform and effective collaboration as the fuel of effective teams
- Continually developing teams *and* individuals
- Viewing collaboration as dependent on learnable skills more than personality
- Expecting excellence in individual performance *and* teamwork

A K–12 Learning School System

Leaders at All Levels

- Developing an urgent and compelling vision to provide all students with a high-quality education (the justice imperative)
- Balancing advocacy with inquiry
- Choosing greatness over maintenance; courage over caution
- Building an inclusive and collaborative work culture centered on core values
- Encouraging leadership that supports the heart and the mind everywhere in the organization
- Creating and sustaining the essential collaborative structures, such as common planning time

Capacity Building for All Educators

- Demonstrating a growth mindset
- Encouraging continual conversations about teaching and learning
- Creating frequent feedback loops
- Continually seeking out external research
- Utilizing and valuing practitioner's knowledge (internal view)
- Developing data teams that analyze problems, research internally and externally, hypothesize, implement, assess, and respond
- Valuing the importance of self-reflection
- Insuring quality supervision and evaluation
- Valuing professional development that is linked to student needs and is the essential resource that fuels individual and team growth

improves. In a K–12 learning organization, "every educator engages in effective professional learning every day so every student achieves" (Learning Forward, 2012).

In this book, we present a model to improve learning for all students by expanding the collective potency of educator talents throughout an entire K–12 school system (including the central office administrators working together with all school-based educators). The model—shown on the preceding page—is based on four high-leverage drivers that will dramatically change the culture in all schools, and lead to vastly more educators inventing better educational solutions for all students on a daily basis. Researcher Michael Fullan states that "an effective driver is one that achieves better measurable results with students" (2011, p. 4).

Unlike programmatic initiatives mentioned earlier, these four drivers are at the core of a high-performing school system. They are the main drivers needed to break the limitations of the past, find new educational solutions, and push the quality of education forward for all students.

The four high-leverage drivers that will enhance teaching and learning are

- **The Importance of Trust (Chapter 3)**

When a climate of trust exists, you can feel it. You know that your colleagues and supervisors care about your success and will do whatever they can to help you succeed. According to researchers Michelle Reina and Dennis Reina, founders of the Reina Trust Building Institute, "Without trust, employees have little interest in being creative, taking risks and collaborating. The generative power begins to wane and performance is diminished. However, trust can be rebuilt after it's been broken" (2007, p. 36).

In Chapter 3, we delve into what leaders can do to build and repair trust between and among educators.

- **Collaboration in All Directions—Elevating the Importance of Teamwork (Chapter 4)**

Almost all school systems can identify their star teachers, who often work in isolation. As the famous baseball manager Casey Stengel once said, "Finding good players is easy. Getting them to play as a team is the hard part." Chapter 4 examines why collaboration is a much more effective strategy than attempting to hire only outstanding teachers. The chapter discusses the multiple ways schools can create and foster educator collaboration in all aspects of school life.

- **Capacity Building for All Educators (Chapter 5)**

In Chapter 5, we will explain why it is essential that every school district build educator capacity every day, even if budgets are extremely limited. The chapter will discuss the traditional model of professional development and its limitations, and a new model that is more likely to increase student learning. The new model is designed to build educator capacity, interpersonal capacity, and organizational capacity to change educator practices and increase student learning.

- **Leaders at All Levels (Chapter 6)**

Hundreds, if not thousands of books have been written about the attributes of effective leaders. In schools, effective leaders espouse a compelling vision that inspires others to work tirelessly to accomplish common goals. In Chapter 6, the definition of school leaders is expanded to include teachers who take charge to improve learning for each other. The chapter discusses the personal qualities of school leaders in a learning organization and ways to develop future leaders everywhere in a school system—central office leaders, principals, department heads, and teacher leaders.

The chart on page 46 lists the details of the four high-leverage drivers. At the center of the chart is a circle labeled *A K–12 Learning School System.* When the four drivers of the model are in place, the culture shifts from isolation, compliance, and standardization to a culture of collaboration, engagement, capacity building, and differentiation throughout the school system.

In Chapters 3 through 6, we will discuss in detail the four high-leverage drivers that must be nurtured in all schools, all at the same time, in order to break from the limitations of the past and enable educators to find better ways to meet the academic and emotional needs of all students.

SYNERGY: WHEN THE FOUR DRIVERS WORK AS ONE SYSTEM

Synergy, as discussed previously, is defined as "a behavior of a whole system *unpredicted* by the behavior of its parts taken separately." While each of the drivers shown on the previous chart can independently improve a school or school system, combining them synergistically as one system will significantly increase the overall impact on adult behavior to improve student learning. The dynamic of a culture of high trust, collaboration in all directions, capacity building, and leaders throughout the organization liberates educators to generate new ways to improve student learning every day.

What happens when the four drivers work as one system? In such a synergistic system

1. *Information flow* between and among teachers and school leaders increases because educators collaborate and trust one another. Educators share day-to-day student performance data, best practices within the school, and best practices from sources external to the school.

2. *Problem-solving abilities* increase when teachers and school leaders work as teammates and trust one another. Collaboration is more likely to lead to new or improved solutions than will solutions developed by individuals working alone.

3. Teacher and administrator *engagement* increases when colleagues work interdependently toward school and district goals. Team members empower and push each other, nurture the emergence of new leaders, and hold fellow members accountable.

4. Teacher and administrator *support* for each other increases when educators trust each other and care about the success of their teammates. Fellow teachers, teacher-leaders, and administrators help one another achieve school and district goals.

5. Teacher and administrator *competencies* increase when teachers and administrators collaborate, solve problems, and share best practices both within and outside the school system.

A graphical representation of the four drivers operating as one system is shown in Figure 2.1. The arrows show that each strategy can increase or decrease the effectiveness of the other three drivers.

For example, suppose there are serious divisions between school board members and the superintendent of schools in the XYZ School System, which just announced its third year of major layoffs without consulting principals. In this scenario, it is highly likely that the trust between the superintendent and the principals would seriously decline, which would then affect the other three drivers in this model—the overall school and district leadership would decline, capacity building would decline as administrators stop supporting each other's work, and the quality of

Figure 2.1 Trust, Collaboration, Leadership, and Capacity Building

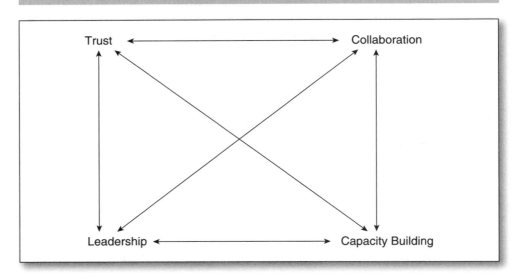

collaboration would decline as central office administrators and principals resist working with one another.

The opposite scenario is also possible. If there is a high level of trust between the superintendent and the principals, then leadership, capacity building, and collaboration may increase. Maximum synergy is reached when all four drivers are positive and increasing.

Earlier in this chapter, we discussed the problem of too many initiatives and initiative fatigue, which is a common problem in many school systems. Here we examine how a K–12 learning organization is more adaptable than a school system that overemphasizes teacher isolation, standardization, regulations, and compliance. We argue that educators who work in a school system with a high degree of trust, collaboration, leaders at every level, and capacity building are better able to choose which initiatives to support and which ones to delay or reject.

For example, in one suburb in the Boston area, the superintendent formed an achievement gap task force to identify how the district could close the achievement gap for students of color. Over the next three years, the task force launched numerous initiatives throughout the school system. Initially, there was great enthusiasm by teachers and parents. However, as initiatives mounted, teachers complained of exhaustion. Finally, the teachers' association president told the superintendent that the teachers supported the goals, but they could not keep up so many good ideas. The union president said that teachers worried that the mission would fail due to initiative fatigue.

Given the level of collaboration and trust between the superintendent and union president, they agreed to form a committee that would study the number of initiatives and their impact. On the day the committee was formed, members began writing each initiative on chart paper pasted on the wall. Within one hour, the committee identified 31 gap-closing initiatives throughout the district.

While the central office had generated only a small number of initiatives, committed and energetic principals and department heads had generated their own gap-closing initiatives. As more and more people generated additional initiatives, the classroom teacher got hit from all sides—more initiatives than even the best teacher could handle.

Given the level of leadership, trust, and collaboration in this school district, the initiative committee members were honest with each other and could address the problems without blaming anyone. After a few more sessions, the members provided the district with a reality check and recommendations to focus their work the next year.

EMBEDDING THE ADULT LEARNING SYSTEMS THROUGHOUT THE K–12 SCHOOL SYSTEM

Another goal of creating a K–12 learning system is to embed the four drivers everywhere throughout the school system so that no matter where you look, you see the same four drivers being used by every team. At the negotiating table, for example, trust, collaboration, and leadership increase each side's ability to generate new solutions to problems (capacity building). The same four drivers are also visible during the budget process when school boards, finance committees, and other important stakeholders openly discuss their needs and how to allocate resources fairly. At the district or school level, when tough personnel actions are required, the central office and principals need to trust one another, collaborate, exercise leadership, and learn together in order to make fair and legally sound decisions. Finally, at the school level, teacher trust, collaboration, and leadership are essential qualities of effective teacher teams (professional learning communities).

To illustrate that an adult learning system requires all four drivers, here are two representative examples—one at the board-to-board level, and one at the teacher-to-teacher level.

BOARD-TO-BOARD COLLABORATION

In 2006, the town manager of Lexington, Massachusetts approached one of the authors of this book, Paul Ash, superintendent of schools, to see if he would be willing to consolidate the municipal and school facility departments in order to save money and improve efficiency. Initially, the superintendent and school board were concerned about the loss of fiscal and operational control, while the town manager and board of selectmen saw advantages if the town created one town-wide operation.

During the next six months, the school board, board of selectmen, town manager, and superintendent of schools engaged in numerous honest conversations about their respective needs and concerns. Unlike in some towns, the parties to these negotiations trusted one another and were willing to explore whether a new, townwide facility department would be more effective than two separate departments. Ultimately, the two boards and two town leaders wrote a memorandum of agreement in 2007 that merged the finances and employees into one department jointly controlled by the town manager and the superintendent of schools. According to town and school officials, the new combined department is now able to provide more differentiated staffing by area of expertise (for example, facilities leadership, energy management, project management, long-range capital planning, and security) at no additional cost.

TEACHER-TO-TEACHER COLLABORATION

In another Massachusetts school system, the teachers were frustrated with the K–5 report card and saw the need to create an easy-to-understand, standards-based report card. Over a period of two years, a group of volunteer teachers and the director of curriculum and instruction looked at standards-based report cards from other school districts to find the best models that could be adapted to their needs. Finding promising models was the easy part. The hard work was writing a new K–5 report card aligned with the district's learning expectations.

During the two-year process, the committee members assumed leadership roles as each academic area was studied, debating with each other on the best ways to measure student progress. This process required high levels of trust, leadership, and collaboration. The intense two-year project increased teacher capacity and made it possible for teachers to design a more effective K–5 report card.

OVERCOMING THE SIX HISTORICAL LIMITATIONS OF THE PAST

In Chapter 1, we described six historical factors that hindered even outstanding school systems from achieving high standards for all students. If we reframe the six limitations in terms of their opposites, it becomes much clearer to see what schools must do to break the limitations of the past and increase educator capacity.

Factors Limiting Learning	Factors Generating Higher Learning
1. Schools designed for some students	1. School designed for all students
2. Mindsets and beliefs that all students cannot learn at high levels	2. Mindsets and beliefs that all students can learn at high levels
3. Standardization	3. Differentiation
4. Teacher isolation	4. Teacher collaboration, leadership, and engagement
5. Limited professional development for all educators, which is not essential	5. Ongoing professional development for all educators, which is essential
6. Teaching and learning as separate acts	6. Teaching and learning as an interactive process between educators and the students

We have seen evidence in school districts that educators will constantly find ways to shift from the limiting factors on the left side of the chart to the factors generating higher learning on the right side of the chart, if the school system builds trust, leaders throughout the district, collaboration in all directions, and capacity building for all educators. This statement is a theory of action, which can be written as an if-then statement—*If X happens, then Y will happen*. If the four drivers of the model are comprehensively enacted, then educators are enabled to break down obstacles of the past and find better ways to meet the academic and behavioral needs of all students.

In order to illustrate how a K–12 learning school system can break the limitations of the past, we show how the model will change schools from a factory (or batch education) model to a dynamic, system model. Listed on the left side of the chart that follows are some of the major characteristics of factory model organizations. On the right side of the chart are the major characteristics of an adult learning model.

Factory Model	Dynamic, System Model
Standardized procedures	Flexible procedures
Independent workers	Interdependent workers
Bureaucratic organization	Team orientation
Top-down leadership	Leadership in all directions

(Continued)

(Continued)

Factory Model	Dynamic, System Model
Centralized control	Decentralized control
Few decision makers	Many decision makers
Compliance	Initiatives at every level
Top-down communication	Communication in all directions
Isolation	Open work environments
Adversarial relationships (union, management, parents)	Cooperative relationships (union, management, parents)
Independent, passive learners	Interdependent, active learners
Teacher has the knowledge	Multiple sources of knowledge

Source: Adapted from Reiguluth & Garfinkle, 1994, p. 6.

Under the factory model, educators are expected to carry out production orders from their superiors and have little or no power to make any decisions. When the culture is based on the attributes on the right side of the previous chart, all educators are empowered individually and collectively to make educational decisions in real time, and do not have to wait for orders from the boss. We contend that a K–12 learning system enables educators to end the factory model of schools that educate batches of students and to create dynamic schools that focus on the needs of all students.

ADDITIONAL THOUGHTS ON THE DRIVERS OF CHANGE AND SYSTEMS THINKING

In a recent paper, researcher Michael Fullan (2011) argued that the United States is focusing on the wrong drivers of change to improve student learning. He claims that focusing on accountability, individual teacher quality, technology, and fragmented initiatives will make matters significantly worse if they are the lead drivers. According to Fullan, the "wrong four drivers de-motivate the masses whose energy is required for success; the right drivers do the opposite" (2011, p. 6).

He urges that countries adopt four other lead drivers that are much more effective, since they "work directly on changing the culture of school systems (values, norms, skills, practices, relationships)" (p. 5). In his paper, Fullan

Drivers That Make Matters Worse	Drivers That Make Matters Better
Accountability: using test results and teacher appraisal to reward or punish teachers or schools	Capacity building
Individual teacher and leadership quality: promoting individual solutions	Group solutions
Technology: investing in and assuming the wonders of the digital world will carry the day	Focusing on the quality of instruction
Fragmented strategies	Integrated or systemic strategies

contrasts the four lead U.S. drivers, which in his opinion will make matters worse, with the four lead drivers that he claims will improve learning.

Fullan's concerns were recently discussed at the April 2011 meeting of the Council of Chief State School Officers in Washington, D.C. Leaders from departments of education throughout the United States assembled to discuss how they can support school districts that will be forced to implement the new Common Core State Standards (45 states, 3 territories, and the District of Columbia), and launch new student and teacher evaluation systems to measure student learning and teacher effectiveness. According to Fullan, there is little evidence that mandating a national curriculum and a teacher evaluation process linked to student test scores will improve student learning (p. 9). The new federal drivers are external to the teacher, will force compliance, and will do little to inspire teachers to create new solutions to help students achieve at higher levels.

Our model overlaps with Fullan's four drivers of effective change. In both cases, we list capacity building and group work (collaboration in all directions) as two of the lead drivers. However, in our model, we add two additional drivers: building and supporting leaders at all levels of the system and creating a climate of trust. While there are both similarities and differences between the Fullan model and ours, both focus on changing internal conditions within a school organization that are directly linked to enhancing and strengthening the culture of the workplace and not on the external conditions imposed by state or federal governments.

In our model, we emphasize that when trust, collaboration, leaders at all levels, and capacity building are present at high levels and work synergistically, the entire school system is better able to break from the limitations of the past and improve learning for all students and teachers.

Based on our experience, we agree that state and federal standardization of curriculum and learning standards may be necessary to ensure educational equity and improve poorly performing school systems. However, further standardization is unlikely to help good systems become great school systems or to produce high results for all students. In order to create highly effective school systems, school leaders must work to create a culture that empowers, supports, and encourages all educators, working collaboratively, to find better educational solutions for all students.

In Chapters 3 through 6, we will take a deep dive into the attributes of the four drivers of systemic change. In these chapters, each driver will be more fully explained from the point of view of a practitioner who is seeking to launch the drivers in his or her school or school system.

3 The Importance of Trust

A superintendent was involved in a negotiation session with the teachers' union to establish a new supervision and evaluation process. The superintendent wanted the new process to be less bureaucratic and more focused on capacity building. He wanted to replace the traditional clinical-observation model of teacher evaluation with a new process in which the supervisor would engage in an in-depth discussion with each teacher about areas where that teacher would like to improve. This new, collaborative conference would focus on problem-solving. When the superintendent proposed this new model to the negotiating team, one of the teachers on the team candidly asked, "Why in the world would I want to discuss with my principal an area where I might be struggling?"

In this story, the teacher expresses distrust of her supervisor and concern that any information she might share about her struggles as a teacher could be used against her in an evaluation. This distrust then carries over to the superintendent as well as the teacher expresses disbelief that her superintendent could ask teachers to put themselves in this vulnerable position. At a deep level, the teacher does not believe that her supervisors have the best interests of teachers at heart.

In order to create a vibrant learning organization in which all staff members continuously work towards professional growth and learning, we must first create a professional culture in which teachers and administrators can admit and discuss their weaknesses with their supervisors or colleagues so that they can receive support and grow. Educators must believe that they are safe with the information they share, and the listeners (including listeners in positions of power) will not hurt them when they share their vulnerabilities. In this chapter, we delve into the attributes of trust in a school system so that leaders can examine ways to think about what they can do as practitioners to build trust within their schools.

WHY IS TRUST IMPORTANT IN A LEARNING ORGANIZATION?

In the 19th century, the one-room schoolhouse teacher taught alone and very rarely met with his or her supervisor. Since these teachers were largely solo practitioners, collegial trust was not a concern. Teachers were responsible for their own learning.

However, unlike the one-room schoolhouse in the 19th century, the average public school today is much larger and employs numerous faculty members with diverse specialties. In these much more complex learning organizations, trust between faculty members is essential, if the goal is to break down teacher isolation and build a professional collaborative culture focused on improved student learning. When there is trust between colleagues, more and more educators are willing to share information, debate with each other, integrate perspectives, and coordinate tasks to improve teaching and learning.

Educational researchers Bryk and Schneider found a strong correlation between schools with high levels of trust and student performance. They examined 100 schools between 1991 and 1996 and found that the schools in the top quartile for standardized test scores had higher trusting relationships, as measured by faculty surveys, than schools in the bottom quartile (Bryk & Schneider, 2002). In a 2003 article, the same authors reported the finding that in 1994 schools reporting strong trust links were three times more likely to report eventual improvements in reading and math scores than those where trust levels were low (2003). Their analyses "document a strong statistical link between *improvements in relational trust and gains in academic productivity*" (2002, p. 116). While correlation does not mean causation, our many years of professional experience bears out this commonsense conclusion—when faculty members trust one another, they are much more likely to work together to improve both teaching and learning.

In their study, Bryk and Schneider describe the *relational trust* between faculty members as a complex dynamic in which parties depend on one another and on a shared vision (2002, p. 30). This kind of trust rests on respect, competence, integrity, and personal regard for others (2002, pp. 23–25). While high personal regard is a necessary ingredient in trust building, Bryk and Schneider note that relational trust reduces the sense of vulnerability that comes with the risk of change and facilitates collective decision making.

We argue that when there are high levels of trust in a school:

- Learning increases for both educators and students;
- There is higher faculty and staff morale;

- There is less teacher turnover;
- The school is more likely to attract higher quality teachers, since people want to work in a system that trusts them and will support them; and
- Faculty members are more likely to work with one another and share ideas.

Additionally, since feelings are contagious within a school, high trust between supervisors and colleagues increases trust within classrooms and students' trust of their teachers, which leads to increases in depth and breadth of student learning.

As school leaders, espousing that we should trust teachers is the easy part. Actually building and sustaining high levels of trust throughout a school are both intellectually and emotionally challenging. In the next section, we discuss what trust looks like in a learning school so that administrators can begin the journey to create a high-trust culture in their school or school systems.

WHAT DOES TRUST LOOK LIKE IN A LEARNING ORGANIZATION?

While *trust* is a word that is used frequently, there often is not a common understanding of what it means. For some, it is related to "walking the talk," when there is a coordination between espoused values and beliefs and the behaviors of those who espouse them. For others, it means a leader allowing teachers to contribute to significant decisions that affect teaching and learning. Tschannen-Moran, from the College of William and Mary, defines "trust as one's willingness to be vulnerable to another based on the confidence that the other is benevolent, honest, open, reliable, and competent" (2004, p. 17).

While the language above is helpful in describing trust in a general way, it is not specific enough for school administrators who would like to build trust in their schools. To assist school leaders with their action plans, we have divided the general concept of trust into four specific areas in a learning organization. This list is nonexhaustive, but serves as a basic framework for approaching this topic. Please note that the four areas of trust are discussed independently in the sections below; however, in practice they are not independent variables—each variable affects the others synergistically. For example, a school leader cannot expect to be trusted as much if they demonstrate only some of the attributes but fail to embrace others.

Listed below are four attributes of trust in a learning organization:

1. Leaders who genuinely care about their teachers' professional growth and success in the classroom.

2. Leaders who model vulnerability and demonstrate openness to continuous learning.

3. Leaders who work through conflict to achieve common goals.

4. Leaders who are willing to lose trust to gain trust.

1. Leaders Who Genuinely Care About Their Teachers' Professional Growth and Success in the Classroom

In the anecdote at the beginning of this chapter, the teacher on the negotiation team probably does not believe that her supervisor genuinely cares about her success in the classroom, which is why she asks, "Why in the world would I want to discuss with my principal an area where I might be struggling?" Additionally, the teacher more than likely would be more comfortable camouflaging what she does not know rather than revealing it.

Imagine what the teacher would have said to the superintendent of schools if she had felt safe discussing with her supervisor areas where she wished to improve and believed her supervisor genuinely cared about her professional growth. If real trust existed between the teacher in this scenario and her supervisor, we suspect the teacher would have welcomed the superintendent's proposal to replace a classroom observation with a structured interview.

The first step in building trust in any school is getting to know your fellow employees. At a very basic and personal level, faculty and staff members are more likely to trust school leaders who take the time to get to know them as whole people, including their work. Building trust is a gradual process, which is why school leaders need to get out of the office more often, walk around the school, visit classrooms, and engage in more conversations with anyone and everyone. As school leaders demonstrate they know more and more about their employees, more faculty and staff members will begin to make the leap to trust their supervisors.

While visibility in the school and "getting-to-know-you" conversations are important first steps in the trust-building process, deeper trust will only be established if employees genuinely believe they are safe, valued, and respected.

Studies from the business world provide insight to what an educational supervisor's work should look like when he or she genuinely cares about teachers' professional growth and motivation. In a classic article in the

Harvard Business Review titled "One More Time: How Do You Motivate Employees," originally published in 1968 and reissued numerous times since, the late sociologist Frederick Herzberg contended that most employees are motivated by intrinsic factors such as achievement, recognition of that achievement, the work itself, and personal growth, and are not motivated by extrinsic factors, such as a boss that will deliver a "kick in the pants" (Herzberg, 1987). Successful school leaders are those who show they care by recognizing and praising their employees' successes, and who create a school culture that values professional growth. Another study by Sirota, Mischkind, and Meltzer found that to maintain enthusiastic employees, management must provide recognition, coach employees for improvement, help the employee get the job done, and instill an inspiring purpose (2006). Both studies reach similar conclusions about how thoughtful managers create healthy, trusting relationships in the workplace.

Building on the work of Bryk and Schneider, we recommend that leaders focus carefully on four interpersonal arenas that are linked to trust building:

1. *Respect*	Acknowledge the important and significant role that each person plays within a school environment (from custodian to department chair)
2. *Competence*	Understand the importance of successfully executing the responsibilities of one's own role and ensuring that everyone else does as well
3. *Personal Regard for Others*	Demonstrate genuine caring for others
4. *Integrity*	Exhibit a consistence between what one says and what one does

When leaders can demonstrate the above four qualities, others begin to experience trust within their work environment.

When supervisors are perceived as serving the needs of all faculty and staff members, trust is more likely to be sustained than when the perception is the opposite, that leadership is detached and uncaring, or that the leadership is unable to understand, acknowledge, or serve the needs of their constituents. Trust is personal, and starts with supervisors demonstrating that they genuinely care about their staff and their staff's success.

2. Leaders Who Model Vulnerability and Consequently Support Continual Learning

Recently, one of us participated in a meeting with three urban superintendents who were discussing how to move their systems forward amidst a dizzying array of obstacles: academic and financial challenges, new statewide and Race to the Top initiatives, and an increasing number of local mandates. Each of these district leaders voiced a wish: if only they could acknowledge publicly that they were not certain about the optimal way to move forward, and that the path to improvement was uncertain. Each of these leaders also expressed that in their communities, admitting their uncertainty was nearly impossible or at least unwise. These administrators maintained that they needed to keep up the appearances of confidence and certainty.

While we understand the potential political fallout when leaders reveal their uncertainties to constituents, we also recognize that leaders who do not show any humility risk losing the trust of their constituents, and lose an opportunity to show these constituents that they, too, are learners. School leaders must be willing to model experimentation; if the leader is willing to take risks, other educators will be more willing to take risks themselves. While some constituents may see the acknowledgment of uncertainty and the need to experiment as an expression of weakness, others will see it as demonstrating courage and humility.

Management expert Patrick Lencioni, in his analysis of effective teams, states that "team members who are not genuinely open with one another about their mistakes and weaknesses make it impossible to build a foundation for trust" (2002, p. 188). Lencioni defines trust as a willingness to be vulnerable within the group. He argues that the ability to be vulnerable and build trust is an important quality within a learning environment. When leaders are willing to model that they too are learners, they send a powerful message to others that none of us knows everything. Their humility and vulnerability builds trust with faculty members and models their commitment to adult learning.

In a learning school system, administrators and teachers must be willing to experiment, take risks, and trust that their colleagues won't harshly judge a short-term failure. In a high-trust environment, educators are willing to admit what they don't know (vulnerability) and accept failure if their experiments do not yield intended results. Not all experiments will succeed. If failure is interpreted as a result of poor performance rather than as part of the ongoing research required to discover successful new approaches, then it is likely that educators will avoid risk or hide less than optimal results.

In Atul Gawande's *Better: A Surgeon's Notes on Performance* (2007), the author describes ingenuity as a requirement for success. Ingenuity is necessary in education, considering the number of unsolved challenges educators face. According to Gawande:

> Ingenuity is often misunderstood. It is not a matter of superior intelligence but of character. It demands more than anything a willingness to recognize failure, yet not paper over the cracks, and to change. It arises from deliberate, even obsessive, reflection on failure and a constant searching for new solutions. (p. 9)

Nondefensive "reflection on failure" in a team setting requires trust of one's teammates and a willingness to be vulnerable with them. In order for educators to nimbly develop new proficiencies and stretch their skills and knowledge, it is vital that they share their vulnerabilities with others and receive constructive feedback and support from supervisors and colleagues. This level of feedback and support will happen only sporadically in an environment where adult learning is not supported and embraced. Most adults can quickly sense when their supervisors will tolerate experimentation in the workplace and the developmental stages of learning and when their supervisors will not. If professionalism is viewed as perfection, then educators will be cautious about trying new strategies and approaches. When professionalism can encompass ongoing learning, adults are more likely to try out new ideas.

The Impact of "Learning Trust" on Student Learning and Adult Learning

When teachers create a climate of trust in the classroom, students are more willing to take academic risks and expose their vulnerabilities because they know that the teacher will not embarrass them. They know their teachers will help them examine and learn from their mistakes. We call this kind of student trust *learning trust.*

Students often worry about "appearing like a fool" in class, making mistakes, or appearing incompetent and untalented. Learning trust develops when learners believe that it is safe to learn—to risk finding a solution, offering an answer, or sharing a thought process. Learning trust is a form of cognitive and emotional safety that undergirds learning.

For many students, schools can be dangerous places to learn. When students do not learn, they often experience poor grades as a form of punishment for not learning. This punishment can then exacerbate students' fears and worries, causing students to avoid risks whenever possible and to stick with "things they are already good at." Schools should be places where young people can learn new skills and areas of knowledge. Educators must address the significant psychological risks students are asked to take when they are challenged to learn new skills and concepts. We must begin to understand the importance of cognitive and emotional safety in all its facets, and to foster it in all students.

While many educators and noneducators alike understand this concept, it often is not applied to the adults in the school environment. New Zealand researcher John Hattie has undertaken a significant analysis of educational research and his work has helped distinguish which interventions and strategies yield the highest impact on student learning (2012). One of those high-impact levers is the ability of teachers (and leaders) to establish a disposition towards errors and mistakes that encourages learning and minimizes embarrassment and shame.

Hattie notes that school "leaders and teachers need to create schools, staffrooms, and classrooms in which error is welcomed as a learning opportunity"(p. 19), and in which teachers as well as students can feel safe to learn, relearn, and explore knowledge and understanding. In such an environment, mistakes are seen as opportunities to correct understanding, not as evidence to make negative judgments about intellectual capacity. When teachers establish learning trust in their classrooms, student learning is strengthened.

From our experiences, it is equally important to establish a similar understanding about errors in the community of educators within a school setting. In order to have adults continually grow, they must work in a climate in which errors can be discussed and analyzed in order to reap the learning that is embedded in them. That is not going to happen, however, in the absence of trust. Learning and trust are intimately connected.

3. Leaders Who Work Through Conflict to Achieve Common Goals

One way that colleagues can demonstrate open and honest communication is through the debate of ideas. People who trust one another are more likely to be able to wrestle with opposing views and enhance their respective thinking and decision making. Trust is a necessary condition that allows people to disagree and offer each other contrasting perspectives and new information. The ability to engage in constructive discussion and debate is essential to the ongoing improvement of schools. This is a habit of mind that is essential to pass on to our students and, in order to do so, adults must model it. We call this *collegial trust*.

Schools abound with conflict. Conflict may arise from any of the differences, diversities, or struggles for power that exist between members of the school community. Conflict may be heated or hidden. It can occur between constituent groups (such as administrators and teachers) or within constituent groups (for example, between students and other students or teachers and other teachers). Some conflicts arise over educational issues, while other conflicts arise from noneducational issues (such as finance, safety, discipline, race, ethnicity, or religion), and if not managed well, can limit a school's ability to educate students.

Part of the responsibility of school leaders is to identify, understand, unpack, manage, and resolve conflict so that it neither lies dormant and erodes morale, nor erupts explosively, damages relationships, and impedes teaching and learning. When important matters are not discussed openly, they don't go away. Often the "real" conversations and opinions leak out in the parking lot after the meeting or in small groups in corners throughout the building. However, within the seeds of disagreement and conflict often lie ideas and perspectives that can improve schools and school cultures and lead to innovations that can improve learning or school climate. School leaders must approach conflict as a way to both build trust within the school community and to improve the school.

In order to build and maintain trust, school leaders must develop the skills and processes to identify, diagnose, and manage conflict in their schools. Parties in conflict look to their leaders to create a safe "container" for the conflict, in which they are heard, listened to, respected, and understood, and in which they feel confident that the leader will not retaliate against them for their views or honest expressions of their feelings. Leaders must communicate openly and honestly, keep their word about confidentiality, and demonstrate willingness to make difficult decisions. They are not fearful—successful leaders view conflict as opportunity, and can comfortably "sit in the fire" of conflict. Trust develops and deepens as parties work through the conflict and over time see meaningful improvements in the conditions that led to the conflict.

Leaders who avoid and deny conflict as a way to maintain the appearance of harmony will foster school cultures in which conflicts remain buried, passively corroding confidence in leadership. When leaders fear and avoid conflict, teachers and staff may keep "pretending" to get along with one another, while harboring anger towards and distrust for one another. Leaders must acknowledge conflicts within their schools and develop an organized process for engaging them productively, or teachers and staff may become cynical about leadership and lose trust. Faculty may begin to feel that there will be no change in "the way we do things around here."

When there is conflict about an educational issue, rarely will teachers engage in an open and honest debate that surfaces strong emotions. Many teachers will remain passive during faculty meetings, allowing one or two more senior or powerful teachers to argue for the status quo without questioning or challenging their ideas. Teachers may remain silent because they are averse to conflict by nature or because they worry that a heated argument may damage their relationship with colleagues. Faculty members may also decide to remain silent out of worry that expressing their views will damage their relationship with a superior or even cost them their jobs.

We believe that without open and honest dialogue, administrators and faculty members will not be able to work through conflicts to improve the school or school system.

4. Leaders Must Be Willing to Lose Trust to Gain Trust

Recently, a principal in a Boston suburb decided not to renew an assistant principal's contract. In another school, the principal decided not to grant tenure to a new teacher completing his third year at an elementary school. In a third school, the principal did not select a very popular and effective teacher who applied for an internal department head position. These three decisions all caused significant pushback from faculty, parents, or both.

In the first case, teachers were quite upset because the assistant principal was well liked and had provided them with significant support. In the second case, parents were upset because they saw this young teacher as someone who had very strong relationships with their children. In the third case, colleagues could not understand how someone who was so admired within the school could not be selected for a leadership position (here, the department head). In all three cases, the principals knew that their personnel decisions would not be embraced by the faculty or parents but nonetheless made those decisions based on what they believed was in the best interest of students.

Such courageous decisions are usually unpopular and will often temporarily reduce the level of trust between the principal and the staff. In all three cases, the principals had the trust of their teachers before they made these tough personnel decisions. However, after the decisions, the teachers lost trust in the leader; they expressed anger and disbelief and questioned the principal's judgment. These three stories illustrate the plain truth of leadership: Tough personnel decisions can adversely affect the overall level of trust within a school or community.

While it is true that making tough personnel decisions may reduce the faculty's trust in their school leader in the short term, it is also true that if a school leader makes all decisions based on the needs of the school (and not on the leader's individual needs), trust in the leader may eventually be restored and grow over time as faculty members see that their school leader has integrity and courage. There is no fail-safe way to prevent certain personnel decisions from damaging or reducing trust; ironically, school administrators who lack the courage and conviction to make difficult decisions to improve their schools may lose faculty trust anyway.

As all principals and superintendents know, faculty and parent trust in them will increase or decrease over time, depending on their latest decisions. For example, when a leader makes a popular decision, faculty morale and trust is likely to increase. When a leader makes an unpopular decision that is seriously challenged by one or more constituent groups, trust is likely to decline. However, school administrators can reduce the impact of tough personnel decisions when they demonstrate respect, competence, integrity, and personal regard for others.

There are many different kinds of difficult decisions that school leaders have to make (for example, financial, personnel, programmatic, and policy decisions). While there are no actions that will automatically restore trust, paying attention to the emotional state of the community is an important part of the healing process after a difficult decision, and this attentiveness will ultimately contribute to the revitalization of the learning system. Many decisions, including personnel decisions, have a huge emotional impact on both school administrators as well as on faculty members. We offer the following advice to school leaders for reducing the negative emotional impact and loss of trust that result from unpopular decisions:

1. Explain why the decision was made (respecting confidentiality in personnel cases);

2. Be as open and honest as possible;

3. Acknowledge the pain, loss, anger, and impact of the decision; and

4. At all times, demonstrate genuine concern for others.

When the teachers and parents feel that their views and feelings are genuinely respected, it can go a long way in slowing down the erosion of trust. Teachers and principals want to know their leaders are truthful and care about their well-being. It is our experience that trust will be maintained and restored if, over time, the leader's behavior demonstrates thoughtfulness, care, concern, and regard for the employees, students, and parents.

In the preceding sections of this chapter, we focused on the importance of trust in an adult learning organization. In the next section, we will discuss the importance of trust in the classroom and why teacher-student trust is one of the essential elements of effective teaching and learning.

HOW TO BUILD TRUST

How does one build trust? Trust is usually built bit by bit in small increments that are additive. "Atoms" of trust can be built by careful listening and attentiveness to what people are saying and also to what they are feeling. Trust is also built through authenticity, such as when a person acts congruently with his or her values, and through honest communication that is delivered respectfully. Even when delivering criticism and challenging feedback, the respectful school leader communicates respect for the ability and intelligence of his/her teachers.

Roger Weissberg and others have written that academic achievement of students is linked to the strength of their emotional connections to the school environment (Zins, Bloodworth, Weissberg, & Walberg, 2004). Their research establishes that classroom and school interventions that make the learning environment safer, more caring, better managed, more participatory, and that enhance students' social competence increase student attachment to school. Students who are more engaged and attached to school have better attendance and higher graduation rates, as well as higher grades and standardized tests scores. Bryk and Schneider's research on relationship trust established a similar link between adult affiliation to colleagues and student achievement.

Reina and Reina's analysis of trust formation (2007) is in accord with this view. They provide a list of factors that make people more, or less, likely to trust others:

We are inclined to trust people . . .

- who are self-aware
- who take responsibility for their role in the relationship
- who demonstrate that they consider the best interests of others rather than just themselves
- who do what they say they will do
- who practice the values they tell us are important to them
- who are willing to recognize and consider both sides of the story
- who listen and respond to our needs and interests
- who are willing to think about what they have to give as well as what they hope to receive

We are not inclined to trust people . . .

- whom we experience as selfish and self-absorbed
- who do not demonstrate an interest in the needs of others
- who are not willing to accept responsibility for their actions
- who gossip or talk about others behind their backs
- who blame others without looking at their role in the experience
- who make snap judgments and draw conclusions before hearing all the information
- who are not open and receptive to the ideas and views of others; people who consistently feel that they know all the answers and their way is the only way and the right way
- who change the rules all the time
- who are inconsistent in their behavior so we don't know what to expect from one interaction to the next
- who distort the truth by omitting information for their own purpose

What is apparent from these tips is the overlay of emotional intelligence that is inherent in the behaviors that generate trust: self-awareness, taking responsibility for one's behavior, being sensitive to the needs of others, being a careful listener, open-mindedness, and being authentic by acting in congruence with one's espoused values. These behaviors demonstrate a grasp of the social and emotional skills that are critical to effective communication and continuous learning, for both adults and students, within a school or school system. Emotional support and understanding is one of the foundational building blocks of trust within classrooms and the larger school environment.

HOW TO FORMATIVELY ASSESS THE LEVEL OF TRUST

Trust is as important a factor to measure within a learning school environment as the achievement data that is such an essential marker of educator efforts. While we are still learning how to develop reliable measures of qualitative assets such as trust, we strongly recommend the regular use of a template such as the one below that contains the agreed-upon attributes of trust and a means for community members to rate how that attribute is reflected in their own experiences. Collecting such formative assessments about the vibrancy of the climate, especially as it relates to trust, in combination with transparently communicating the results of such analysis will further underscore the importance of this lynchpin to continual learning.

TRUST WITHIN THE SCHOOL COMMUNITY

Attribute	Rating 1–5 5 is high	Comments
How well do leaders support the needs of teachers and students?		
How well does communication address issues openly and honestly?		
How consistently do members of the community engage in difficult conversations around important topics where there is disagreement or misunderstanding?		
How well is conflict embraced as one means of developing common understanding and commitments to important matters?		
How well does the work environment (culture) support the learning of both students and educators?		
How consistently do members honor and follow group norms?		

We also recommend utilizing the following five items, which come from Bryk and Schneider's Teacher Trust Scale (2002, p. 157; see also Tschannen-Moran, 2004, pp. 198–199).

On a 1–6 scale, with 6 equating to strongly agree and 1 equating to strongly disagree, how well do you agree or disagree with the following statements:

1. Teachers in this school trust each other.

2. It's okay in this school to discuss feelings, worries, and frustrations with each other.

3. Teachers respect other teachers who take the lead in school improvement efforts.

4. Teachers at the school respect those colleagues who are expert at their craft.

5. Teachers feel respected by other teachers.

While using either template will not provide a statistically valid portrait of trust within a setting, the information gleaned will be very helpful in promoting important conversations and dialogue about this vital arena.

TRUST SYSTEMWIDE

In a high-functioning learning organization, trust is a critical attribute between and among all school constituents: between students and teachers, between teachers and principals, between principals and central office staff, between the superintendent and the school board, between educators and parents, and between school officials and community members. In order to build trust throughout a school or school system, leaders must value, support, and model

- Caring relationships between and among all school constituents, and
- Open and honest communication combined with careful listening (strengthens the quality of relationships more than avoidance and cursory listening).

When these principles are followed consistently, trust emerges. Once trust is established, the conditions for continual improvement are established.

A longitudinal analysis of successfully restructuring schools concluded that

human resources—such as openness to improvement, trust and respect, teachers having knowledge and skills, supportive leadership, and socialization—are more critical to the development of professional community than structural conditions. . . . The need to improve the culture, climate, and interpersonal relationships in schools has received too little attention. (Bryk & Schneider, 2003, p. 41)

Trust that emerges from caring relationships and open communication is one of the factors that will expand the limitations of our current structures. Trust is not just a positive human emotion that improves working and learning conditions. Trust is a lynchpin of improved achievement.

CLOSING THOUGHTS

While school systems without trust can produce successes and have programs that are exemplary, trust is one of the four drivers that sustain continual growth. It both provides a safety net that supports ongoing experimentation and research and fuels the system's capacity to address unanticipated problems and obstacles that arise from the inevitable misunderstanding and conflicts that are part of complex communities. Trust is necessary for the system to achieve beyond its current capacity.

It is also important to note that, while the ultimate goal of schools is to produce competent and caring students, this is not going to happen without paying attention to the needs of educators. We believe that some of the recent national debates have created a false dichotomy between the needs of adults and the needs of students. Serving both sets of needs is essential to the workings of a learning school system.

4 Collaboration in All Directions

Elevating the Importance of Teamwork

Without collaborative skills and relationships, it is not possible to learn and to continue to learn as much as you need to be an agent of societal improvement.

—Michael Fullan (1993, p. 18)

When educators work collaboratively toward the same goals, they increase the capacity of the school and school system to improve learning for all students. Most U.S. schools, despite their modern appearances and student access to computers and the Internet, still operate as a collection of single-room schoolhouses (classrooms). In typical schools, teachers' schedules, labor contracts, and evaluation measures focus on the work of individuals rather than the work of teams. The school system's infrastructure reinforces the efforts of the individual and does not value the collective work of the group. Additionally, even when a district is able to marshal some resources to allow individuals to work as a team for part of a day, teachers can still face formidable obstacles from colleagues, administrators, unions, and parents to implementing changes proposed by their teams.

Other books focus on the impact of individual collaborative teams within schools (sometimes known as *professional learning communities* or PLCs), but we argue that isolated PLC groups are only the first step to forming a school or systemwide learning organization. In a larger learning organization, teachers and administrators must collaborate in all directions in order to raise the capacity of all educators to effectively educate students. Collaboration in all directions means that within each school and throughout the district every educator collaborates with others consistently in order to develop more effective educational approaches.

While some readers may already be convinced that collaboration is a powerful driver of improvement in a school system, we recognize that other readers may be skeptical or unconvinced because of their own experiences when they have been asked to collaborate with colleagues. For those readers who have enjoyed working on teams and found the collaborative work beneficial, we hope this chapter will help you to identify additional ways to improve the quality of collaboration in your work setting. For those readers who remain unconvinced, we acknowledge at the start of this chapter that it is very difficult to make the transition from a school that values teacher isolation and autonomy to a school system that values collaboration. We acknowledge that some readers may have found teamwork frustrating and sometimes a waste of time. We also recognize that we have the burden of proof to convince you that a culture of collaboration in all directions is more effective than a traditional school, particularly when traditional school districts already meet state and district standards.

In this chapter, we unpack the attributes of effective collaboration—describe what it looks like and what it requires. We provide a blueprint for how to develop more highly functioning partnerships and teams. If successfully supported, collaboration will help educators gain access to the creativity and cognitive horsepower that is latent within effective, collaborative teams. Collaborative teams are a powerful source for increasing achievement for all our students. By more clearly defining effective collaboration and ensuring that educators have both the time and the skills to collaborate, schools and school districts will gain access to a steady stream of innovative and imaginative strategies that will improve student achievement.

WHAT IS COLLABORATION?

Each year, thousands of people run the Boston Marathon. Men and women run 26.2 miles from the small town of Hopkinton to downtown Boston, Massachusetts. While all of the participants run in the same direction and have the same goal, they are not a team. They are a group. Group members work independently and team members work interdependently. In a school setting, teachers working alone in their classrooms are solo practitioners working on independent goals, while teachers on collaborative teams work interdependently to achieve common goals.

In their study, researchers Rick and Becky DuFour, along with Robert Eaker, who are experts on PLCs, define collaboration as a "systematic process in which we work together, interdependently, to analyze and impact professional practice in order to improve our individual and collective results (Fullan, 2008a, p. 3). In their definition, they highlight three key attributes of effective collaborative teams: they are systematic, they require interdependent work, and they are results oriented. In PLCs, teachers systematically meet and work together as teammates, in order to improve their capacity to more effectively educate students.

These three attributes are found at the core of all effective teams in schools: departmental, school, and interdistrict teams. At whatever level of the school system teams are established, effective teamwork requires that individuals learn from each other, generate new ideas, and solve complex problems.

WHY IS COLLABORATION IMPORTANT?

Numerous studies show that U.S. teachers strongly support greater collaboration in schools. In 2009, MetLife conducted a study of 1,003 public school teachers and 500 principals in grades K–12, and reported that 67% of teachers and 78% of principals think that "greater collaboration among teachers and school leaders" would have a major impact on improving student achievement (Metlife, 2009, p. 9). The study concluded that teachers in schools with higher collaboration

- are more satisfied with teaching as a career;
- are more likely to strongly agree that teachers, principals, and other school professionals at their school trust one another;
- are more likely to strongly agree that other teachers contribute to their success in the classroom; and
- believe more of their students have a sense of responsibility for their own education. (p. 19)

In a 2010 survey of 40,000 teachers conducted by the Bill & Melinda Gates Foundation and Scholastic, 86% of teachers identified a collegial work environment as "absolutely essential" or "very important" for their persistence in the profession, and 89% reported time for teachers to collaborate as "absolutely essential" or "very important" for their persistence in the profession. Similarly, in a recent survey conducted by Berry, Daugherty, and Wieder for the Teachers Network (and supported by the Ford Foundation), the authors found that 68% of the 1,210 teachers in the sample acknowledged that they turned to other teachers for help about teaching, and 74% reported that they turned to other teachers for support (p. 11). In addition, close to 80% of respondents concurred that their involvement in the Teachers Network was a major reason for their intention to remain in the teaching profession. These findings underscore the importance of opportunities for teacher collaboration and the role of collaboration in teachers' commitment to their vocation (Wei, Darling-Hammond, & Adamson, 2010).

In 2008, a Teaching and Learning International Study (TALIS) of teachers in high performing nations (Australia, Austria, Belgium [Flemish Community], Denmark, Estonia, Ireland, Korea, and Poland) found that just under 50% of a teacher's time is spent in the classroom and a substantial amount of time is set aside for teachers to collaborate. In contrast, American teachers spend most of their workweek teaching classes, with about 2.7 hours per week allocated for collaborative activities such as common planning time (Metlife, 2009, p. 9). Despite teacher support for collaboration, few school communities have fully actualized the significant potential in this domain. The same study found that only 16% of teachers surveyed agree that there is a climate of cooperative effort among staff members in their schools (Wei et al., 2010, p. 20).

Given that changing any large institution is difficult, why should school leaders bring about change to increase collaboration in U.S. schools? Research overwhelmingly shows that educators throughout the country respond that more collaboration will increase collegial trust, job satisfaction, teacher success in the classroom, and student responsibility for their own education (Fullan, 1993; MetLife, 2009; Mourshed, Chijioke, & Barber, 2010).

Based on our years of experience leading schools, we have identified five additional advantages of collaboration in schools:

1. improved quality of teaching

2. increased organizational sustainability

3. increased organizational adaptability and better solutions to complex educational problems

4. increased organizational consistency and accountability

5. increased collective capacity to educate all students

Collaboration is most evident in the work of effective, high-functioning teams. However, we see collaboration as a broader concept that includes teams and other networks that demonstrate the three DuFour characteristics we mentioned above.

Five Additional Advantages of Collaboration

1. Collaboration increases the *overall quality of teaching.* Hiring the most brilliant, hard-working, effective teachers who work in isolation will never lead to high achievement for all students. When teachers work within teams, they can more effectively share information and best instructional practices, analyze student work, and develop strategies to improve the quality of teaching. In collaborative teams, teachers are better able to learn from one another, accommodate weaknesses, and provide support for new and veteran teachers. In one of the largest studies ever conducted in the field of education, involving a synthesis of over 50,000 studies and 800 meta-analyses of student achievement, John Hattie drew one major conclusion: "The remarkable feature of the evidence is that the biggest effects on student learning occur when teachers become learners of their own teaching" (2012). In collaborative teams, teachers support, challenge, and stimulate each other, enhancing teacher learning.

2. Collaboration increases *organizational sustainability.* When a high-quality solo practitioner resigns or retires, his or her skills and knowledge are lost. In effective teams, however, skills and knowledge are more distributed, so that when one person leaves, less colleague and institutional knowledge is lost. Additionally, when teachers work in teams, new teachers can more quickly learn school expectations and history from colleagues.

3. Collaboration increases the *organization's ability to adapt* and to solve *complex educational problems.* When teachers work in isolation, the flow of important information between and among teachers is reduced, limiting the number of faculty members who can solve problems and adapt to school needs. However, when teachers work in high-functioning teams, they share information with each other, analyze problems, and generate new ideas more effectively than individual thoroughbred teachers working alone. Teachers who work in inter- or intradistrict teams can produce powerful ideas and significant positive change both in schools and in an entire school system. Schools today must adapt to a changing world and solve complex educational problems on a regular basis.

4. Collaboration builds intra- and interschool *consistency, predictability, planning, and accountability.* When collaboration increases within schools

and across the school district, teachers and administrators share knowledge about all aspects of the school system. Shared knowledge is the first step toward more consistency, predictability, planning, and accountability.

5. Collaboration increases the *collective capacity* of all educators. When all educators collaborate, they share knowledge with each other, which increases the collective capacity of the overall organization. According to Michael Fullan,

> The power of collective capacity is that it enables ordinary people to accomplish extraordinary things—for two reasons. One is that knowledge about effective practice becomes more widely available and accessible on a daily basis. The second reason is more powerful still—working together generates commitment. Moral purpose, when it stares you in the face through students and your peers working together to make lives and society better, is palpable, indeed virtually irresistible. The collective motivational well seems bottomless. The speed of effective change increases exponentially. (2010, p. 72)

The concept of collective capacity is more fully discussed in the next section.

NONE OF US IS AS SMART AS ALL OF US

High-functioning teams can solve complex problems at much deeper levels than can individuals working alone. In the world of science and engineering, the concept that the whole can be greater than the sum of its parts is known as synergy. Inventor Buckminster Fuller's favorite illustration of synergy was the behavior of the alloy chrome-nickel steel, whose extraordinary strength at very high temperatures enabled the development of the jet engine.

> Its primary constituents—iron, chromium, and nickel—have tensile strengths of 60,000, 70,000, and 80,000 pounds per square inch respectively, and combine to create an alloy with 350,000 psi tensile strength. Not only does a chain made from the alloy far exceed the strength of its weakest component, but counter-intuitively even outperforms the sum of its components' tensile capabilities. (Edmondson, 2007, p. 40)

The concept of synergy also applies to teams in the workplace. Synergistic, high-functioning teams in any discipline are smarter than the sum total of their membership. Education is no exception—high-functioning teams of educators, working to solve complex educational problems, will perform better than high-quality individual teachers working alone.

Keith Sawyer, in his book *Group Genius,* describes how collaborative efforts, constant conversation, and side-by-side work led to synergistic breakthroughs such as psychoanalysis, impressionism, and quantum physics which "emerged over many years of interactions, trial and error, and false starts—not in a single burst of insight" (2007, pp. 8–9). David Freeman of CBS News reported another example of synergy at work in teams. He described how teams of online game players were recruited to decipher the molecular structure of key protein retroviruses similar to HIV/AIDS. He noted, "Nonscientist gamers came up with an accurate model of the so-called protease molecule in three weeks. Biochemists had been trying to create such a model for more than a decade." During three weeks of play, the gamers generated over a million structure predictions. The solution, reached by the winning team in 10 days, was nearly perfect (2011).

While a minority of teams act synergistically, many stumble in their practice. For some people, negative teamwork experiences lead them to believe that teamwork is neither helpful to instruction nor beneficial to student learning. (As the maxim attributed to automobile designer Sir Alexander Arnold Constantine Issigonis has it, "A camel is a horse designed by a committee.") We all know, based on personal experience, that it is not enough to just put people into teams and then assume their members will function at a high level without ongoing support.

Before school administrators launch large-scale collaborative activities in their schools, we recommend that they take the time to develop with their faculty a shared understanding of collaboration in the school or school system. In the next section, we discuss three of the major shared understandings we believe must be in place before there can be a major shift from a culture of autonomy and isolation to a culture of collaboration.

DEVELOPING A SHARED UNDERSTANDING OF COLLABORATION

School leaders must provide educators working on collaborative teams with clear expectations and ongoing supports as part of the process of building highly effective, collaborative, synergistic teams to advance student learning. Specifically, we think it is vital that leaders

1. Establish a clear vision of effective collaboration;

2. Acknowledge that collaboration is not easy, and that there will be challenges; and

3. Communicate openly about changes that will occur.

1. Establish a Clear Vision of Effective Collaboration

Developing a common understanding of what constitutes a high-functioning team and what effective collaboration looks like is the most important step needed to shift schools from a near-total focus on the individual educator to a combined emphasis on individual expertise and group effectiveness.

In the workshops that we conduct, we often ask leaders to think of a team in their school. Once they select that team, we ask them to decide whether the team is high-, medium-, or low-functioning. After this exercise, we ask each workshop participant to describe to a partner why they chose a particular level of functioning. In listening to administrators describe their criteria for assessing the team, we find that there is rarely a common understanding across a district as to what constitutes a high-functioning team. Some of the criteria we hear relate to congeniality (members get along well), a sense of common purpose, or inclusivity. Some of these behaviors are clearly important to team functioning. However, across a room filled with administrators from the same district, what is rare is a common set of criteria that are linked to the importance of innovation and achieving breakthroughs that individuals acting alone could not achieve.

While every school will need to establish its own vision for effective collaboration, and the needs of every team are different, we have listed below attributes of teams that in our experience are central to their effectiveness:

- Supportive and distributed leadership
- Shared values and vision
- Collective learning and the application of that learning to practice
- Mutual trust
- Outreach to partnerships and networks beyond the school for sources of learning
- Reflective dialogue
- Transparent practice

Once a shared understanding is in place, professional development must support the acquisition and strengthening of necessary team skills.

2. Acknowledge That Collaboration Is Not Easy and That There Will Be Challenges

Leaders must acknowledge that collaboration usually includes some degree of discomfort. The discomfort can come from loss of autonomy, personal time, or individual control; confusion over tasks, responsibilities, and deadlines; or from clashes of goals, values, and perspectives. It is essential that school leaders acknowledge that even for the veteran educator collaboration is not a comfortable old shoe.

Moving from a focus on individuals to teams requires a shift towards greater collective responsibility. Guidance counselors, adjustment counselors, special educators, teachers of the arts, wellness instructors, Pre-K teachers, and other school personnel all play a significant role in student success. However, these educators do not often work closely with academic classroom teachers. Collaboration in all directions is not just about grade-level teams or subject-matter departments, but also about all faculty members working together as teammates toward a common purpose. This transition from a focus on academic classroom teachers to increased collaboration with other school faculty and shared responsibility for student outcomes can be very challenging for some faculty members.

Discomfort does not arise solely from the changing relationships between academic classroom teachers and special subject teachers. Some of the most confident and experienced academic classroom teachers can be thrown into anxiety and self-doubt if they are asked to change their grade level or subject area the following year, even if they are licensed in the new area. These changes mean the teacher will leave an assignment in which he or she is confident and enjoys a high degree of independence and move to a new setting where he or she will be the inexperienced teacher in the subject matter or age group and more than likely will require frequent support from other teachers. If the teacher is also expected to collaborate with colleagues, he or she will go from being the "expert" with colleagues to a "rookie" with much less knowledge and will feel dependent on others and sometimes vulnerable.

One of the authors recently had a medical experience that provided some insight into the sometimes oppositional perspectives on collaboration found in schools. In order to successfully manage the effects of a complicated surgery, the author had to move from independence to dependence. For a short period of time, he became reliant on a range of medical specialists and assistants and lost much of his ability for self-care. Being dependent on the group left the author feeling both vulnerable and angry. The anger derived from the loss of independence and the vulnerability engendered by the fact he had to rely on the skills of other group members, in addition to his own contributions, in order to achieve the goals that had been set for his recovery. Despite a previous commitment to and an embrace of collaboration as a concept, the author did not feel that this new approach was progress; in fact, it felt very much like the opposite. Ultimately, the net effect of this team approach proved successful—the patient got healthy— but during the process, the author felt resistant to it.

In schools that have for many decades derived success from the accomplishments of individual educators, a move towards interdependence and collaboration will prove challenging. While such a change may seem logical to some, it will also evoke both anger and vulnerability.

Collaboration also requires that schools move away from what author and consultant Elisa MacDonald describes as a "culture of nice" (personal communication, 2010). Effective collaboration requires that educators work through clashing values and perspectives. Disagreements, as well as moments of discord and discomfort, are a necessary stage if partners and teammates are going to develop new approaches and strategies. Effective collaborators will need to have some difficult and intense conversations about those topics on which they disagree. This kind of conflict can be quite uncomfortable for some educators. It is critical that leaders both acknowledge this normal stage of collaboration and provide support and skill-building instruction in how to constructively engage in conflict management and difficult conversations. In the section of this chapter on conflict transformation we will discuss how administrators can help teachers work through conflict with colleagues.

Too few educators have actually experienced working on a high-functioning team where the final product far exceeds what individual efforts might have created. Until school leaders can help educators in their districts build a track record of positive collaborative experiences, they will encounter considerable skepticism and cynicism.

3. Communicate Openly About Changes That Will Occur

As a school or school district moves from teacher independence to collaboration and interdependence, many structural and cultural changes will occur. School leaders must be open and transparent with faculty about these changes.

Structurally, schedules and contracts will have to change. Educators cannot collaborate effectively with one another if they are squeezing team time into and around the current structures of schools (for example, if time for collaboration is only possible after school). School leaders need to set aside significant time during the school day for educators to meet and collaborate. In order to accomplish the shift to collaboration in all directions, school schedules and structures will have to change to make room for teamwork.

We have listed below some important ways administrators can change schedules and structures to support collaboration.

- Examine the teachers' contract to determine if there are ways to create collaborative time within the existing contract

- Schedule teachers who teach the same courses or grade levels to the same planning and preparation periods (this does not work for teachers who teach singleton courses)
- Hire substitute teachers for teachers who need to collaborate on a project or participate in team professional development
- Allocate some after-school department or faculty meeting time for collaboration
- Allocate some in-service days for collaboration (if they exist)

The above examples alone are unlikely to permit sufficient time for teachers to collaborate with other faculty members (K–12 teams and cross-functional teams). This is why superintendents must be willing to change schedules (in nonunion states) or to bargain for such changes in states with collective bargaining.

In addition to structures, attitudes and beliefs will also change in schools that shift from a culture of independent teachers to a culture of collaboration. For example, in a school that values the individual teacher and individual excellence, it is common to hear parents and teachers say that the most important work takes place when teachers are teaching in the classroom, not when teachers meet during the day or during an early release day. However, in a school that makes the transition to a collaborative culture and the benefits of collaboration are well accepted, the culture of the school shifts from one that values only teacher autonomy to one that values both quality teaching in the classroom and the work of collaborative teams.

Schools that shift to a culture of collaboration also experience a leveling of hierarchy. In collaborative schools, all teachers are valued contributors to improving student performance and the school climate, not just the academic teachers. Additionally, in collaborative teams, all teachers, veteran and novice alike, are equal members. New teachers have increased access to information and support from veteran teachers, and veteran teachers can learn from the perspectives of teachers who were more recently trained. In a hierarchical model, veteran teachers have most of the power, and new teachers may be to some degree silenced. A collaborative model allows for better decision making with regards to student education and school climate because all perspectives are more consistently valued and included.

WHAT ARE THE LEARNABLE SKILLS OF COLLABORATION?

The skill sets required for effective teamwork are both teachable and learnable. Most educators are steeped in the knowledge of individual pedagogy, yet many schools have not provided the time, structure, feedback, or professional development around effective team practice. While numerous schools have initiated PLCs, Inquiry Teams, Data Teams, and Child Study Teams, they have not necessarily provided these teams with the training and support they need to enable them to function effectively, let alone synergistically. Some recent surveys of educators show both a positive attitude towards collaboration *and* a sense of frustration with how that collaboration is experienced.

A number of school administrators have shared with us that teams in their schools demonstrate a wide range of effectiveness. Some are highly focused and participants work well together, while other teams struggle. As one educator reported, "Teams have a casino quality to them. Sometimes, we get lucky and the combination of personalities clicks. At other times, the group is non- or minimally functional." In our observations of schoolwork, we see and hear of repeated instances of teams that are struggling with functionality. Administrators often feel powerless to alter the dynamics of teams by any means short of removing individuals who are perceived to be problematic or adding high-functioning members into weaker group settings. Although there are times that these approaches can, in the short term, have an impact on group performance, they are not the only options to improve team performance. The substitution approach usually will not succeed in changing a dysfunctional team into a high-functioning mode, and removing people from teams can have a long-term negative impact on organizational culture and trust.

In *Group Genius*, Keith Sawyer points out that "managers who have embraced the power of collaboration have largely taken a black-box approach: They look at overall team characteristics—such as members' personality traits—instead of investigating what goes on inside the box" (p. 174). While congeniality among groups may improve professional relationships, personality traits alone are not sufficient to enable teammates to solve difficult problems or to innovate.

Many people experience the process of effective teamwork holistically, as a kind of "group flow." Sawyer defines group flow as a "state of peak performance that groups reach, when the members blend together just right, and the environment allows a certain kind of focus and concentration on the work" (Burkhart, 2007). The term *flow* was coined by Mihaly Csikszentmihalyi, head of the psychology department at the University of Chicago. However, an analysis of group dynamics that centers only the holistic experience and does not delve down into the granular elements that make up interactions between teammates will not be maximally useful for practitioners trying to foster more effective teamwork in their schools. Feedback is as important to team members as it is to individual teachers. Teamwork skills such as managing conflict and developing and adhering to norms and protocols in order to optimize performance can be strengthened by the feedback of both team members and outside observers. Teamwork skills are best taught at the granular level, by identifying each problematic pattern or interaction in the team, and intervening to improve it. As we shift from a focus on individuals to teams and other collaborative structures, it will also be important to shift professional development and other supports such as supervision to the collaborative networks within the school community.

School leaders need to encourage and provide careful attention to the creativity of school teams. Inspiration and innovation have to become expectations of our collective efforts.

We recommend that you ask yourselves if currently your school's ability to achieve its goals is consistently enhanced by collaboration? If the answer is "No," the underlying issues blocking such synergy must be addressed. As it is unacceptable to ignore a poorly executed lesson, it is equally unacceptable to ignore a team that is not exceeding the productivity of what an individual member could achieve.

In this section, we describe five key skills that will help raise the probability that the work of educators will gain synergy from collaboration. These skills come from a review of research on group effectiveness in combination with decades of experience observing teams functioning within schools.

1. Careful listening—Teammates need to be able to summarize both what people are saying and what they are feeling. On effective teams, team members listen carefully and value listening as much as speaking as a vital team resource. This kind of listening allows members to build on each other's ideas. Implied in this skill is equality; that is, each voice is of the same importance and thus must be heard. Also embedded in careful listening is the idea that each participant's perspective is limited and that by seeking the points of view of others the member gains expanded vision and knowledge.

2. Conflict transformation—Teammates see conflict as a resource and not as an obstacle. The aim is to navigate through conflict rather than avoid it. In many school groups, a culture of politeness often obstructs conflict management. On other teams, some individuals dominate while others remain passive as a means of dealing with conflict.

The teams that transform rather than avoid conflict will often forge new understandings that will increase productivity. In the book *Difficult Conversations,* Douglas Stone and his colleagues identify the following major skills for engaging in a difficult conversation: acknowledging feelings, responding to criticism with curiosity, distinguishing intentions from impact, and replacing blame with a mapping of the contribution system (Stone, Patton, & Heen, 2000).

Typically, conflict involves competing values and perspectives. When such conflicts arise, many educators either shy away from the dissonance or engage in a debate in which one side tries to prove its case. On effective teams, team members acknowledge the conflict and engage in learning conversations. For example, team members use the difference in opinions to listen carefully and attempt to first understand what separates the viewpoints. Members of such a team would not act as if one person or one group possessed the truth. Rather, team members would act as if each person had a limited view and that a difficult conversation would produce aspects of the problem that could not be seen at first.

The *transformation* occurs when engaging in the conflict leads to new insights or understandings that are more nuanced than those originally perceived. In Chapter 6, we will discuss this important aspect of effective teamwork as an equally important factor in what contributes to skillful leadership.

3. Improvisation—Teammates build upon a diverse array of perspectives to develop a new direction, a new plan, and a new strategy. School groups that are facile with improvisation value the importance of raising questions and understand that questions are as vital as initial answers. Questions will sometimes force a team to reframe problems, potentially saving them from adopting an incomplete or ineffective solution. Also, part of embracing improvisation is accepting the idea that new approaches are not guaranteed successes. There might be as many failures as triumphs when it comes to strategic interventions to improve learning. The key to effective improvisation is the team's ability to nimbly respond to data that suggests that a particular strategy is not working. It is careful attention to the impact of a particular approach on student learning that generates the need for improvising an alternative approach that adjusts to the emerging needs of learners.

4. Norm adherence—Teammates are willing to shape, follow, and value norms that govern participants' behavior while on the team. We list below a sampling of team norms that promote the kind of high-functioning collaboration we have described in this chapter. You will note that the norms are different from some of the more common rules of engagement developed by many teams, which often focus on organizational issues such as start and stop times or issues related to agendas and note taking. Norms are critical to high-functioning teams. Without explicit attention to issues like disagreements, inclusion of minority views, and balanced participation, over time, teams move away from the behaviors that are linked

to innovation. We highly recommend that teams examine the following list of norms so that they can have an understanding of the kinds of behavior that increase innovation and the chances for group flow.

- *We expect disagreements with our colleagues; the dissonance is part of making sense of this complicated endeavor called education. Treat our differences as a potential resource.*
- *We will disagree agreeably. Learning to be honest, direct, sensitive, and nondefensive is probably the hardest collaborative skill to master. It is worth the effort, however, because when we collaborate, we increase our chances of creating solutions to our problems that are far more powerful than the ones we come up with on our own. None of us is as smart as all of us.*
- *We will balance advocacy with inquiry. Be as interested in other perspectives as your own.*
- *We will listen for the quiet voice and reach out to those who don't speak quickly in groups.*
- *We will monitor personal airtime. The group is large and our time is short.*
- *We will encourage the asking and raising of tough questions.*
- *We will be willing to engage in conflict and stay engaged until resolution.*
- *We will lean into discomfort.*
- *We will take responsibility for what is troubling us and for sharing it with appropriate persons.*
- *We will treat the candor of others as a gift and honor confidentiality.*
- *We will share our feelings in service of getting to a better place.*
- *We will take risks, make some mistakes, and then let go.*
- *We will try to see the other's perspective and to listen without judgment.*
- *We will listen, listen, and listen.*
- *We will pause and gather data before engaging and judging. We will be open-minded.*
- *We will check for understanding and agreement.*
- *We will encourage full participation.*

While the selection of key norms is a vital aspect of developing high-functioning teams, the establishment of norms must be coupled with ongoing *check-ins* that assess norm effectiveness. Are members following the norms? Are the norms the right ones? Do we need to add or change any? The development of norms that are designed to guide and encourage key behaviors, when coupled with a tenacious and continual checking in to ensure that the norms are alive and well and not just window dressing, provides a sense of safety for all participants. It is that safety zone that allows for the development of trust. That trust will allow participants to be vulnerable, ask for assistance, and take the risks that are inherent to fostering creativity.

5. Peer Accountability—In effective teams, members hold each other accountable as they work interdependently toward the same goal. When the team is functioning at a high level and is meeting its goals, colleagues frequently check in with each other about the work and any obstacles that arise before someone is unable to make a deadline or complete a task. On effective teams, when unforeseen circumstances arise and team members fail to carry their load or meet expectations, other team members can openly and honestly express their concerns and expectations, and the team can determine the best way to move forward. High-functioning teams have strong peer accountability throughout the teamwork process, both when expectations are met and when they are unmet.

Unlike supervisor-to-teacher accountability, where the supervisor has formal power, peer-to-peer accountability is much more difficult to enforce due to equal status and power. Attempting to hold a colleague accountable can be emotionally very difficult and frightening, since most teachers have not been taught how to have difficult conversations with fellow colleagues, nor has the norm been established by group members that everyone on the team has the right to hold each other to team expectations and goals. The skills described above are the same skills that teachers need when speaking with a colleague about team expectations. When the team has established clear goals for itself and expectations for each team member and the group has explicitly established that peer accountability is the norm, this significantly reduces anxiety when one member needs to speak with another about his or her work.

An example of effective peer-to-peer accountability was included in a McKinsey & Company study of effective schools throughout the world:

This is the story of a teacher who joined a primary school that had established the routines of collaborative practice as part of Ontario's literacy and numeracy strategy—these were professional learning communities through which teachers jointly reviewed student learning and developed teaching methods. In that teacher's first week in the new school two of his colleagues visited him and suggested he should use word walls because both found them to be effective. When, two weeks later, he had not yet put up the word walls, his colleagues visited him again, this time urging him more strongly to put up word walls, sitting him down to share why this was a practice in their school and the difference it had made for students. A few weeks later, by then well into the school term, the new teacher had still not put up his word walls. His colleagues stopped by again after school this time simply saying, "We are here to put up your word walls with you and we can help you plan how to use them." As professionals in that school, they has developed a model of instruction that they found effective and which had become hardwired as part of their values (a pedagogy), so they expected others to use it too. Their commitment was to all students and to their professional norms—not just to their own students in their own classrooms—and they were willing to hold each other accountable for using practices that they found effective. Together, the three of them put up the word walls. (Mourshed et al., 2010, p. 75)

Effective teams demonstrate both individual and team accountability. Just as individual members of an effective team must be accountable to each other, the team itself must be accountable to school or district leadership for student results as measured by student achievement data. High-functioning teams use student achievement data to inform, design, and modify educational practices.

Team members will always have a range of capacities and skill sets, and school leaders should not assume that all faculty members know how to function together as high-performing teammates. School leaders should explicitly name and describe the attributes of a high-functioning team, model the behaviors at group meetings, provide professional development to faculty members, and afford formative feedback to individuals and teams. It is not enough for school leaders to say they believe in teacher collaboration and then hope their teachers have the needed teamwork skills. In order to raise the probability that more teams will function effectively, school leaders must set a clear vision and a common understanding of what it means to be a high-functioning team as part of the professional development process.

COLLABORATION IN ALL DIRECTIONS

A major goal of this book is to help school leaders transform their schools from a culture of educator autonomy to a culture of collaboration in all directions. While there are many books that discuss the importance of small-group PLC teams, very little has been written about how to build a K–12 learning school system. We argue that when individuals, PLCs, department teams, school teams, and district teams are interconnected and work toward common goals, student achievement increases beyond what individuals and small groups can accomplish working independently.

As we discussed earlier in this chapter, the first steps for school leaders who wish to take this journey include building a shared understanding of collaboration within each school, providing coaching and support for team members as they develop collaborative skills, and communicating openly with faculty about the structural and cultural changes that will occur. Together, these steps will increase the efficacy both of individual teams within a school and of some teams between schools.

In order to maximize the diffusion of collaboration through a school district, the superintendent and his or her team must model highly effective teams, supervise both individuals and whole teams, and support the K–12 school system with high-quality professional development. The following sections flesh out each of these action steps in detail.

The Superintendent and the District Leadership Team Must Model Collaboration in All Directions

While school systems often can have hundreds of teams operating within their boundaries, the district leadership team, often comprised of principals and central office staff in small to medium districts, or district supervisors and coordinators in larger districts, plays a very influential role in how collaboration is understood and valued within a district. When all the criteria, norms, and behaviors that support collaboration are represented within the district's leadership team, the likelihood is increased that each of the leaders within that team will in turn create and support similar team functioning within their own spheres of influence (administrator-teacher teams and teacher-teacher teams).

Recently, the Massachusetts Department of Secondary and Elementary Education, in collaboration with the Massachusetts Association of School Superintendents, developed a creative approach to inducting new superintendents. One of the central features of this new induction program focuses on the importance of the superintendent developing a highly effective leadership team that models careful listening, conflict management, and creative analysis of districtwide data. In the program, new superintendents are paired with retired superintendent mentors who coach new superintendents on how to develop a strategy to drive reform in the district. One aspect of that strategy is the development of high-functioning leadership teams.

Recently, a new superintendent discovered that in his district there was an issue with ineffective team meetings. A number of principals had organized a variety of teams in their buildings, but they were not functioning at a high level. Additionally, leaders struggled to confront this issue directly. As the new superintendent initiated his own leadership team meetings, he spent considerable time developing norms with participants in a collaborative manner. One of the norms the group had endorsed was to be "fully present" at meetings. Shortly after this norm was established, one of the team members became absorbed in his computer, responding to an e-mail. The superintendent stopped the discussion and asked the participant about the "fully present" norm. The participant responded by saying, "It was an important e-mail." The superintendent noted that the norms would only be viable if they applied to all participants all the time.

The superintendent facilitated this exchange gently. He did not scold or get angry. He simply underscored the importance of adhering to the norms. Modeling this kind of facilitation not only strengthened the functioning of the leadership team, but also illustrated for all participants the importance of addressing issues like this openly and honestly. The leadership team that the superintendent organizes is often one of the most important places where principals and other district leaders learn "how we work around here." Additionally, participating in a high-functioning team is one of the most effective ways to learn how to lead a high-functioning team.

Supervise Both Individuals *and* Whole Teams

School leaders need to expand their supervision to include supporting and evaluating both individual educators and teams as a whole in order to build capacity for both individual educators and for teams. This assessment needs to be consistent and it needs to come from a variety of sources:

- Individual team members need to self-assess, as well as provide feedback on the overall functioning of the team.
- A coach who does not regularly participate on the team should provide regular feedback to the group on how the team is functioning (as measured against the important criteria and norms outlined above) and on how the team can improve.
- Finally, supervisors will need to evaluate the work of the team. This may be the most challenging aspect of team supervision. Highly effective collaborative teams will often develop approaches that do not successfully meet the desired targets. Leadership must understand that in the short term, failure will be an inherent aspect of even high team functioning.

We offer the following checklist of questions for school leaders to consider during the evaluation process, in order to carefully examine the state of collaboration within their districts.

1. How well do educators within the district understand that the main purpose of teamwork is to create ideas and solutions that individuals acting alone could not accomplish?

2. How well do educators within the district understand and demonstrate the important skills and behaviors that contribute to effective collaboration? These skills include

- careful listening;
- conflict transformation;
- improvisation;
- norm adherence; and
- team member accountability.

3. How frequently do teams assess their own functioning? How frequently do teams receive feedback from an outside facilitator about their team functioning? How frequently do teams receive feedback from you (the supervisor)?

4. What kinds of professional development have teams received related to their functioning? Does the professional development demonstrate a clear message that team skills are learnable and not a function of personality?

5. How adequately does the supervision and evaluation system of the district take into account the work of teams as well as individuals?

The third key action step to drive collaboration in all directions is to create more opportunities for all school and district educators to communicate with each other.

Increase Educator Capacity Through a Web of Communication and Collaboration in All Directions

In order to increase the capacity of schools to more effectively educate all students, school leaders need to expand educator capacity through a web of communication and collaboration in all directions. At the district level, by building a robust districtwide professional development program and a districtwide curriculum review process, many more educators will have opportunities to communicate with each other, build shared knowledge, and increase their skills. At the school level, principals should look for opportunities to create interdepartmental teams to address specific needs within the school. These teams could be created as standing committees or temporary committees to address specific, short-term problems. While it is true that schools will continue to rely heavily on the work of individual educators, more and more school districts should also utilize the vast, virtually untapped resource of synergistic collaboration within schools, between district schools, and between colleagues outside the school system.

Collaboration is essential to a learning school system because collaboration spawns innovation. We believe that the vast majority of schools today have not utilized collaboration effectively and aimed its power on the importance of innovation. In the collaborative school organization we envision, every team, regardless of its purpose, needs to be focused on using the power of the group to gain creative insight. Sawyer notes that "when we collaborate, creativity unfolds across people; the sparks fly faster, and the whole is greater than the sum of the parts" (2007, p. 7).

Figure 4.1 is an illustration of a web of collaboration. Similar webs could be created to focus on and center the collaborative connections for students, school department heads, principals, district administrators, school board members, and others. We chose to focus this diagram on teachers because they are the people whose must nimbly diagnose and develop the best educational solutions for students on a daily basis. According to Sawyer, "Collaborative webs are more important than creative people" (2007, p. 185). We agree.

Figure 4.1 Collaboration in All Directions

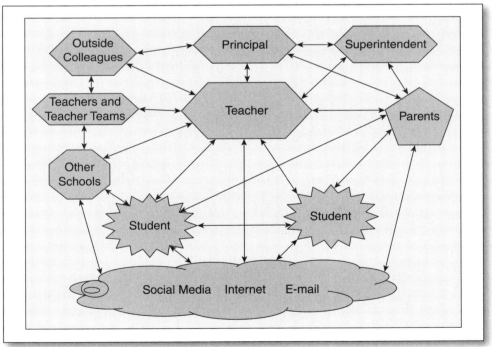

A FINAL NOTE

Strengthening teams in order to gain synergistic collaboration also requires the three drivers we introduced earlier in the book (trust, capacity building, and leadership). When team members trust one another, they are much more likely to collaborate. Trust, as we described in Chapter 3, is founded on the capacity of participants to be vulnerable—to expose their weaknesses and to be open to assistance.

In Chapter 5, we will discuss the importance of capacity building as an essential driver that improves both individual and collective work. Teamwork skills can be isolated and taught. If the prevailing belief system remains that team skills are innate, and that some people have these skills while others don't, adult development will be limited and student achievement will be diminished. In Chapter 6, we will discuss the importance of developing leaders at every level of a school system. Leadership, like team skills, is not simply innate; over time, everyone on the team can be a leader.

5 Capacity Building for All Educators

In Chapter 4, we discussed how collaboration is one of the key drivers that will improve both teacher and student learning. In this chapter, we focus on other ways schools and districts can increase teacher learning so as to expand their capacity to increase student learning. We discuss why schools need to change from the traditional model of teacher professional development, one that is primarily based on individual teacher needs, to a new, more effective model of professional development based on what teachers need to learn in order to identify and address student needs.

Before describing the advantages and disadvantages of different models of professional development, we will first discuss three underlying assumptions of all professional development programs:

1. The quality of teaching in the classroom has a positive impact on student learning;

2. Teaching competencies can be taught; and

3. Professional development programs can increase teacher competencies in ways that will result in increased student learning.

THE QUALITY OF TEACHING MATTERS

As almost every parent knows, the quality of the teacher in the classroom has a large effect on student learning. In two studies that examined teacher quality and its impact on student achievement, researchers in Tennessee and in Dallas, Texas found that effective teaching has a dramatic influence on student achievement (Mendro, 1998; Wright, Horn, & Sanders, 1997).

- Teachers produce a strong cumulative effect on student learning. For example, students placed with highly effective teachers three years in a row beginning in third grade scored 52 percentile points higher (96th versus 44th percentile) on the Tennessee state mathematics assessment than did students with comparable achievement histories who were placed with three low-performing teachers.
- Data from Dallas show that if a student has a high-performing teacher for just one year, the student will remain ahead of peers for at least a few years of school. If the student has an ineffective teacher, the influence on student achievement is not fully remediated for up to three years.

In another study, Darling-Hammond examined the effect of poor quality teaching on student performance and determined that "teacher quality variables appear to be more strongly related to student achievement than class sizes, overall spending levels, [or] teacher salaries" (2000, p. 32). Since it is well established that the quality of teaching in the classroom is strongly correlated with student achievement, school districts cannot simply rely on hiring the most effective teachers; they must also look for every opportunity to support ongoing teacher professional development that focuses on continuous improvements and leads to increased student learning.

EFFECTIVE TEACHING IS COMPRISED OF MANY LEARNABLE SKILLS

Teaching skills can be taught, which is why every state requires prospective public school teachers to complete a licensure program that includes minimum standards for subject area knowledge, pedagogy, and classroom student teaching experience. These licensing standards are based on the widely held belief that there is a body of subject knowledge and teaching skills that all prospective teachers must learn before they enter the profession in order to ensure that all students are taught by qualified teachers. On a national level, Congress passed the No Child Left Behind Act of 2001, that required all public school teachers of core academic subjects (English, reading, language arts, mathematics, science, foreign languages, civics and government, economics, art, music, history, and geography) to meet the "highly qualified" requirements of the Act by the end of the 2005–2006 school year.

While it is true that public school teachers enter the profession with a license from their states, many school systems recognize that new teachers need to further develop their teaching skills. In these school districts, new teachers are required to participate in some form of an induction or mentoring program. For example, new teachers are often paired with experienced colleagues as mentors, and veteran teachers are asked to teach the new teachers skills such as classroom management, lesson planning, and teaching and assessment practices.

The journey from first-year teacher to expert teacher requires many years of practice, reflection, conversations, collaboration with colleagues, and in-depth study. Teachers are learners, which is why almost all teachers continue to take graduate courses and school- or district-level professional development to deepen their content knowledge and teaching skills throughout their entire careers. Teachers understand that educating all students at high levels is complex and requires that they engage in lifelong study of both content and effective classroom pedagogy.

EFFECTIVE PROFESSIONAL DEVELOPMENT IMPROVES STUDENT PERFORMANCE

In 2005, the Australian government produced a report that examined the research on the link between teacher development and student learning outcomes (Meiers & Ingvarson, 2005). The report acknowledged that while there is limited research that demonstrates the direct impact of teacher professional development on student learning outcomes, some recent studies show a linkage. The Australian study and other studies included in the final report provided some conclusions about professional development programs that positively affected teacher knowledge, practice, efficacy, and student learning outcomes.

The Australian government in 2002 studied 70 Australian schools engaged in whole-school professional development. The sample included 42 primary schools and 28 secondary schools. The authors of the study "reported levels of *follow up, content focus,* and *active learning* were all related to the level of impact on teachers' knowledge. The level of active learning was also directly related to impact on teachers' practice and efficacy" (Meiers & Ingvarson, 2005, p. 2). The study reached six major conclusions:

1. It is essential to define student learning broadly and to avoid narrowing outcomes only to those that can be easily measured.

2. Successful professional development programs include opportunities for teacher reflection, collaboration, and building of professional community that contribute to the strengthening of teachers' capacity to improve their students' learning outcomes.

3. Evaluation of the programs over the entire school year may not be sufficient. A teacher taking up new practices may see evidence of improvement in students from an early stage, but it may be two to three years until the new practices are firmly embedded in his or her teaching and evidence can be collected that shows sustained difference in the students' learning.

4. It is important to use a wide range of evidence to evaluate programs, including anecdotal evidence from teachers. Teachers' informed observation of their students over time provided nuanced insights into ways of improving student learning.

5. Evidence suggests that professional learning programs with a strong content focus as well as an emphasis on other features such as follow-up, active learning, feedback, and professional community are likely to show evidence of improved student learning.

6. The level of school support was associated with the extent to which participants in the professional development program found that they had opportunities for active learning. The difficulty in finding adequate time for planning, reflection, and collaboration was an ongoing theme in interviews with teachers. (pp. 91–92)

The study by Meiers and Ingvarson included additional research by C. L. Thompson that investigated the impact of professional development on teaching practices and student outcomes. Thompson found convergence in research that contributed to classroom practice and student performance by

- Focusing on subject matter learning
- Linking professional development to curricular materials and assessments
- Extending activities to permit more active learning, and promoting collective participation to enhance coherence (p. 14)

In his 2001 study, Supovitz reached similar conclusions:

Together, these studies provide a solid basis for concluding that professional development that is connected to specific standards for student performance based upon intensive and sustained training around concrete tasks, focused on subject matter knowledge, and embedded in a systemic context is likely to be effective. (p. 82)

In the same year, Garet and colleagues reached the same conclusions:

> That sustained and intensive professional development is more likely to have an impact, as reported by teachers, than is shorter professional development [and also] that professional development that focuses on subject matter (content), gives teachers opportunities for "hands on" work (active learning), and is integrated into the daily life of the school (coherence), is more likely to produce enhanced knowledge and skills. (Garet, Porter, Desimone, Birman, & Yoon, 2001, p. 935)

In all of these studies, the researchers claim that effective professional development must be coherent, consistent, systemic, and sustained.

Since most of the readers of this book are practitioners, we will now focus on specific professional development practices in schools. We will first define and discuss the traditional professional development model and why the model has had only limited impact on teacher and student learning. We will then present a new model for professional learning based on what researchers have learned about effective professional development as well as on our lifetimes of professional expertise. We propose that the new model achieves three major goals: It allows educators to guide their own professional learning goals, it fosters the development of collaborative and creative relationships with colleagues, and it increases student learning outcomes as defined by school and district goals.

THE TRADITIONAL PROFESSIONAL DEVELOPMENT MODEL

The traditional professional development model in most school districts is teacher-focused rather than being centered on student learning outcomes. Teachers select after-school professional development courses and workshops based on their own preferences and personal criteria, not necessarily based on what they need to learn to more effectively increase student learning. In the traditional model, teachers expand their knowledge and skills predominantly through external programs: college and university courses, seminars offered by experts, and programs offered by professional associations. Typically, school districts approve courses for salary lane credit based on a minimum grade from an accredited college or university.

During the regular work year, teachers are rarely required to engage in professional development activities aligned with school and district goals for more than a few hours to a few days per school year. According to a

2011 article in *Education Week*, "Historically, administrators have favored the workshop approach, in which a district or school brings in an outside consultant or curriculum expert on a staff-development day to give teachers a one-time training seminar on a garden-variety pedagogic or subject-area topic"("Professional development," 2011).

The traditional model typically includes two approaches within a single school district: the internal (district- or school-sponsored programs), and the external (courses, seminars, and programs). The two approaches are described below.

Internal, District-Sponsored or School-Sponsored Professional Development

A typical approach is for the central office to offer a broad range of courses and workshops that teachers can choose from using their own selection criteria. A catalogue usually is distributed to teachers, who can then select programs that meet their personal professional development needs or hours required for relicensure. Some programs may be offered with full college credit, which allows most teachers to apply the credits for future salary advancements. The purpose of the menu approach is to offer all teachers a wide range of voluntary educational programs throughout the school system.

Unfortunately, the districtwide menu approach on its own is a poor vehicle for improving teaching practice and student learning. A study by Joyce and Showers shows that fewer than 15% of teachers implement new ideas learned in traditional staff development programs such as workshops (1996, 2002). While such programs may increase faculty awareness on key topics or teach very narrow, easily-learned skills, short-term programs rarely affect student learning outcomes, since

- the length of each program is not sufficient for teachers to learn complex material or skills well enough to apply them in their teaching;
- courses taken by individual teachers rarely increase team, department, or school capacity;
- programs are not usually designed to provide follow-through support to the teacher after the workshop or course;
- workshops or courses are rarely monitored to assess the program's impact on teacher behavior or student learning; and
- the menu approach does not ensure linkage between what programs teachers choose to take and what skills or knowledge teachers need to learn in order to better meet identified student needs.

Courses, Seminars Offered by Experts, and Programs Offered by Professional Associations

Teachers by their very nature are learners. Since school districts cannot be expected to offer teachers sufficient expert, in-depth professional development, teachers will continue to need to enroll in college and university courses, seminars offered by outside experts, and programs offered by professional associations. These external programs can provide teachers with specialized knowledge that small or moderate-size districts could not offer through their professional development programs. Since most U.S. teacher salary scales reward teachers for credits earned beyond a master's degree (master's plus 15 credits, master's plus 30 credits, etc.), there is also a financial incentive for teachers to take graduate courses.

In school systems with a traditional professional development model, we see the following advantages and disadvantages when teachers take courses or programs outside the school district.

Advantages

- Teachers can take whatever courses or workshops they want.
- The programs allow teachers to develop specialized knowledge and skills that the district cannot offer.
- Teachers can learn from highly respected leaders in their fields.
- Teachers can learn with educators and noneducators outside their school districts.
- Administrators can select courses based on perceived needs for the district's students.

Disadvantages

- Courses may or may not directly connect to school or district needs or to the student needs within a teacher's classroom or assignment.
- Few school districts have sufficient course approval criteria to determine if the learning outcomes for college courses are aligned with what teachers need to learn in order to more effectively address student needs in their own classrooms or assignments.
- When only one teacher from a school or district takes a course, there is limited diffusion of knowledge and skills from one teacher to other teachers, and it does not lead to capacity building within a school or throughout the district.
- College and university courses sometimes lack practical application that could be gained from other modes of delivery such as

job-embedded professional development with consultants working with teachers and students in real time.

- The use of current salary schedules with salary lane changes linked to the number of graduate credits earned is very expensive. A study conducted in California in 1986 found that the average direct expenditure on professional development was $1,360 per teacher (Corcoran, 1995). When investments made by individuals and the present value of future salary increments were included, the investment per teacher was over $4,000. In today's dollars, if a 30-year-old teacher who will work 30 more years earns 15 graduate credits and changes salary lanes worth $1,500 per year, the 30-year district cost, in present dollars, is $45,000 ($1,500 for a 15-credit lane change × 30 years = $45,000). Without clear criteria linking the course approval process to school or district goals, the additional graduate courses may or may not lead to increased student learning.

In the next section, we will discuss a new model of professional development that is designed to provide teachers with high-quality professional development aligned with student needs. The new model is designed to build individual capacity, collective capacity, a culture of curiosity, and a synergistic learning environment. The professional development program is designed to support the mission and vision of the district, and to be aligned with all curriculum and instructional goals.

A NEW PROFESSIONAL DEVELOPMENT MODEL

Unlike the traditional teacher-focused professional development model, the new model focuses on student learning and student outcomes. By that we mean that courses and programs outside the district are approved based on student-centered district standards. Internal daily activities range from required programs closely aligned with major school and district student needs to voluntary programs and activities designed by teachers to enhance their professional skills and thereby improve student learning.

The new model is both a tight fit and a loose fit, depending on the mode of professional development. When the district is responsible for overseeing professional development inside and outside the school system, school leaders apply district-developed standards to tighten the link between the professional development activity and student needs. District and school programs are designed by highly-respected teachers and administrators to expand teacher capacity, based on identified best practices and student needs. At all other times, educators are free to collaborate with colleagues anywhere and at any time to share knowledge, create knowledge, solve problems, refine programs, and innovate. Professional development under the new model is designed to foster a culture of reflection, conversation, collaboration, and commitment to continuous improvement for all educators.

In the new model, professional development is one component of a larger system that is aligned with curriculum goals, instructional practices, and the ongoing assessment of student needs. According to Fuhrman and Odden, one cannot measure the effects of professional development unless there is "alignment of clear and ambitious goals, together with such indicators of results as coherent educational standards, excellent teaching and sound measures of student achievement" (2001, p. 60). While we agree with Fuhrman and Odden that professional development programs must be aligned with clear goals, we do not support a linear program development approach of the sort shown in Figure 5.1.

Figure 5.1

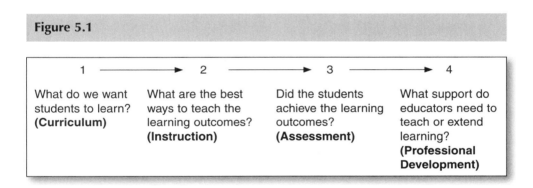

Although a backwards design model is logical, expert creative teachers don't think in linear steps. Great teachers and leaders can get their innovative ideas from anyone, based on a reexamination of the curriculum, instruction, or assessments, in any order, at any time. A linear, backwards design model is not robust or adaptable enough to generate new knowledge and creative solutions in the classroom. This linear design model would most likely be top down, lack flexibility to adjust to new needs in real time, and not foster a joy of learning throughout the school system.

The new model we propose includes professional development as one part of a larger, interactive system that includes curriculum, instruction, and assessment that is always focused on student learning needs. Please see Figure 5.2.

Figure 5.2

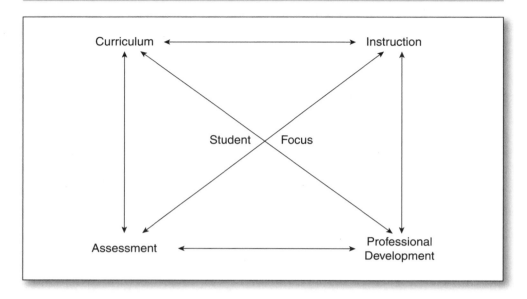

In Chapter 2, we discussed the powerful synergy created when the four drivers of change (trust, collaboration, capacity building, and leadership) work as one system. (See Figure 2.1.) The same is true when the goals of curriculum, instruction, assessment, and professional development are all aligned and focused on desired student learning outcomes. Not only is each component of the system a discipline by itself, each component is affected by the other components. For example, consider the following scenario.

Synergistic Model

Four third-grade teachers are concerned that their students are having difficulty learning some topic or skill. However, the four teachers cannot agree on why the students are not performing well enough. The teachers, who trust one another, debate whether the main problem is the quality of the curriculum materials, the lessons they have designed, the instructional practices they have used, or the quality of their formative assessments. After a period of thoughtful discussion in which they look at the curriculum, their instruction, and their assessment as one system, they all agree that each component could be strengthened; however, they decide that the most important way to go forward is to reexamine how they differentiate instruction. Based on the team's decision, two teachers decide they will enroll in the district's course on differentiating instruction in the classroom to expand and refine their skills, one teacher says she will look for supplemental curriculum materials for the struggling students, and the last teacher says she will plan the next lesson keeping in mind the needs of the students who had difficulty in the prior lesson.

In the preceding scenario, each teacher began the discussion by looking at curriculum, instruction, and assessment all at the same time, rather than looking at each domain as a separate topic to be discussed independently. In their analysis, they understood that making a decision to change any one domain would affect another. If the instructional approach is changed, then the curriculum materials and assessments may need to change, which could affect future professional development needs for the group. The interaction among the team as they made hypotheses and debated with one another was also a form of professional development. As the teachers pushed each other's thinking and shared ideas, the capacity of team members and the group as a whole increased.

When schools view curriculum, instruction, assessment, and professional development as part of one fluid system focused on student needs, educator decisions are more malleable and adaptable to current conditions in schools. Planned and unplanned conversations can lead to amazing new ideas and excitement as colleagues discover new strategies and skills from peer interactions. These conversations can also lead to the identification of new professional development programs, which is central to a K–12 learning organization.

In the prior section, we recommended that educators work to improve student learning by thinking about curriculum, instruction, assessment, and professional development as one larger, interactive system. In sections that follow, we will shift the focus of discussion to two capacities that are required for school districts to maximize student learning, and why the two capacities must also work synergistically. The two capacities are the personal capacity of individual educators and the interpersonal capacity of educators working as a team toward student learning goals. In the final sections of the chapter, we will focus on the three specific ways school leaders can expand educator capacity in their schools and throughout the school district.

Our model for capacity building extends the work of professors Mitchell and Sackney (2000), who claim that personal capacity and interpersonal capacity are two pivotal capacities that need to be built if a school or district is to function as a learning community. These two capacities focus on expanding the repertoire of skills that educators possess and increasing their ability to develop new strategies and approaches to solve educational problems. We strongly endorse their view that "within a learning community, the learning of the teachers is as important as the learning of the children" (p. 2).

BUILDING PERSONAL CAPACITY

Mitchell and Sackney define *personal capacity* as "an amalgam of all the embedded values, assumptions, beliefs, and practical knowledge that teachers carry with them and of the professional networks and knowledge bases with which they connect" (2001, p. 6).

In order to increase personal capacity, educators need to be reflective about their assumptions, beliefs, and mindsets, with respect to both their own and students' capacity to learn. In schools, many of these assumptions are often invisible and rarely if ever discussed, studied, or adapted. For example, if a teacher believes that a group of students is not intelligent or able to learn, that assumption can affect student achievement in several ways, including the extent to which students and staff will persevere when faced with difficulty and setbacks.

Educator assumptions about student intelligence will influence many aspects of their practice, including

- how students are grouped for instruction;
- the level of expectations they communicate to students;
- how teachers respond to their own errors and mistakes as teachers; and
- whether they will persist with all of their students, including those who may not understand a concept the first time it is taught.

Furthermore, the fixed beliefs that adults hold about their own ability to learn can keep them from improving their professional practice. Imagine if all educators in a district believed that regardless of their background and ability they could improve their practice, expand their repertoires, and become more effective. Educators with these beliefs would experience less resistance, challenge themselves to learn new knowledge and skills, and would be more likely to embrace professional growth with a sense of excitement, interest, and enthusiasm.

It is our contention that a "growth mindset"—or the belief that one's skill set can continually increase—can inoculate a school community against the defeatism that can easily overtake an overtaxed system. The role of educational leaders is to help adults examine their beliefs about intelligence, with the goal of motivating themselves and their students to redouble their efforts and experiment with strategies for success. Much of this work stems from the research of Carol Dweck, who discovered that individuals often respond in one of two ways in the face of setbacks. One approach is to become critical in the face of defeat and blame circumstances, others, or oneself (for having insufficient ability). Dweck describes this response as flowing from a *fixed mindset*. Dweck noticed that there is also a different response to disappointment and poor results—the individual seeks out alternative strategies, increases effort, and persistently strives to solve the problem or reach the goal. Dweck describes this approach as emanating from a *growth mindset*.

At the heart of *personal capacity building* is the axiom that all adults within the community are capable of adding to their current skills, learning new ways of approaching instruction, and developing new strategies for working with student needs. In a learning school system there is a growth mindset, and continuous improvement is one of the district's core purposes. If this assumption or norm is not in place, school leaders will rely on hiring and dismissing staff to build needed capacity and will often avoid challenging teachers to grow in new directions.

While most school leaders espouse the belief that most staff members are open to growth and development, sometimes actions speak louder than words. When we discuss team functioning, for example, we frequently hear from building administrators a belief that certain staff members are not able to function effectively in groups, don't listen well, avoid conflict, or simply do not follow group norms. From these descriptions, we discern a sense that things won't change much and that these behaviors are immutable. We sometimes detect similar hidden assumptions when we discuss concerns with special educators within a school setting. We often get the impression that behind the scenes, some special educators are lobbying to assign their students to teachers who adapt well to special needs and are desperately trying to avoid teachers who are not adept at working with students on educational plans. When we question these staff members on their beliefs about whether individual educators will or can change, what we perceive is a sense that this kind of growth or change is highly unlikely.

If the adults in a building don't believe that either they or their colleagues are capable of developing new skills or expanding their abilities, this may become a major obstacle preventing or delaying the community from becoming a learning school system. Furthermore, we believe that if the adults don't see themselves as capable of learning new ways and new approaches, students often will exhibit a similar set of beliefs limiting their growth and development.

Consequently, at the heart of *personal capacity building* is the conviction that all adults are capable of lifelong growth and development. This is the lynchpin of the entire community's growth, and most importantly, the growth of the student members of that community. In a learning school system, school leaders are committed to building personal capacity for new and veteran teachers—content knowledge, pedagogical skills, team-building skills, and leadership skills (without necessarily assuming a typical, hierarchical administrative trajectory). School leaders understand that student success depends on what educators know and can teach.

In Chapter 4 on collaboration, we discussed how individuals working alone are less effective than colleagues working together in teams. Increasing interpersonal capacity between and among all staff members is the second capacity required to build effective schools.

BUILDING INTERPERSONAL CAPACITY

We describe the dynamics involved in shifting from the individual to the team in the chapters on collaboration and trust. The shift requires that individuals demonstrate interpersonal capacities that include active listening, communication skills, conflict management, group decision making, empathy, and respect and care for fellow colleagues. While some staff members come to school each day with these skills already in place, there are others who neither have the critical skills nor the will to work with others to achieve better results for our students.

Mitchell and Sackney note:

> Building interpersonal capacity shifts the focus from the individual to the group. At the core of this component lies collegial relations and collective practice. . . . What this signifies is that the construction of professional knowledge is no longer the solitary pursuit of one individual. Instead, it is a heavily contested process of negotiation among different people with different knowledge bases, different histories, different hopes and aspirations, different personal styles and emotions, and different desires and needs. (2001, p. 4)

If a school system establishes a clear belief in the ability of individuals to build interpersonal capacity, *and* if district leadership provides opportunities for educators to learn or strengthen these interpersonal skills, then the likelihood that individual educators will learn the new skills is significantly increased. One of the best ways that school leaders can teach other educators more effective interpersonal skills is to model the skills in all interactions. In addition, school leaders need to supervise teams and team members for their interpersonal skills, and provide them with feedback in just the same way that supervisors are expected to provide feedback to individuals.

As schools make the transition from a culture of autonomy to a culture of collaboration, the interpersonal capacities of all educators become more important. In schools of the future, educators, students, administrators, parents, and others will spend far more time communicating and collaborating with one another than they do in schools today. The level and means of communication and collaboration will be increased not only by technology but also, and more importantly, by the time educators spend engaged in face-to-face, real-time conversations about student learning and educational practice (for example, data teams, professional learning communities, lesson study groups, child study teams, curriculum review committees, and professional development programs).

While formal structures are essential for meetings and common planning time, there also have to be numerous informal opportunities for educators to share ideas and develop new solutions to complex problems (Sergiovanni, 2000). In schools, one of the most common and most potent ways for educators to collaborate is through conversations that are sometimes planned and sometimes unplanned—anywhere, anytime. The nature and frequency of these conversations will influence the collective capacity of the organization.

High-functioning cultures promote and embrace a set of core values that represent what the school and school district stand for. While core values can vary from one locale to another, respect is a central value in all thriving cultures. Respect is built upon a commitment to open and honest communication. People are committed to disagreeing agreeably and understanding that the dissonance of disagreement often produces new knowledge and ideas. A core value of respect tolerates disagreement, embraces the challenging of ideas, and supports the questioning of positions in a manner that maintains professional dignity for all who are involved in the process.

For the remainder of the chapter, we will discuss four specific approaches that practitioners can use to expand educator capacity, based on research and our own experiences: (1) courses and workshops that are external to the school district, (2) conversations with colleagues within the school district (planned or unplanned), (3) using feedback processes to increase capacity, and (4) programs that are offered within the school district. Unlike the traditional professional development model, these growth opportunities combine both district-directed professional development tied to school and district goals and total educator freedom to collaborate with colleagues in order to share knowledge and skills, create new knowledge, solve problems, and improve practice. Within the model, district programs are mandatory when they need to be and recommended at other times, while most of the time the programs are voluntary.

Courses and Workshops That Are External to the School District

Like the traditional model, the new model encourages educators to take courses and workshops outside the school district when the school system is not able to offer specialized or expert training needed by educators to improve their practice. However, unlike the traditional model, the school district limits outside courses for course reimbursement or salary lane credit to those courses that meet district standards linked to student learning or relicensure. While each district will need to establish their own standards, we recommend the following four standards:

- Courses that will enhance a teacher's knowledge or pedagogical skills in his or her curricular area or grade level. For example, college courses are approved by the school district based on the alignment between the course objectives and what knowledge and/or the teacher expects to learn in order to more effectively meet students' learning needs
- Courses that are aligned with the teacher's professional growth plan for relicensure
- Workshops or seminars offered by external professional organizations when the school system is not able to offer specialized or expert training that educators need to improve their practice
- Courses that are offered by an accredited educational institution (with the requirement that teachers receive a grade of B or better)

Conversations With Colleagues Within the School District (Planned or Unplanned)

Author David Perkins describes how conversations "are the virtual neurons that bind individuals into a larger-scale cognitive collective" (Perkins, 2003, p. 37). He refers to building collective capacity as *creating intelligent organizations*. While every school has conversations occurring throughout the workday, it is the type of dialogue that is occurring that either supports or represses continual growth, and either strengthens bonds or weakens connections among and between individuals. The pace of improvement will depend on how consistently daily conversations among members of the learning community contribute to creative problem solving and true collaboration.

If a school leader could hover over a school district and observe conversations for patterns in a learning school system, he or she would see exchanges that add to ideas, complicate people's thinking, and inspire new insights. In order to raise the frequency with which this level of discourse takes place, conversations must contain more *connected elements* (Perkins, p. 170). The chart that follows provides examples (and counterexamples) of these elements.

Connected Elements	Fracturing Elements
Asking clarifying questions, rephrasing	Dismissing or ignoring ideas, or purposefully derailing innovative ideas through questioning that would lead to their dismissal
Probing, eliciting implicit assumptions	Asserting that there is only *one way* to accomplish something
Testing ideas publicly	Defending positions rather than hearing concerns
Welcoming feedback, taking it seriously, discussing it	Extolling a steady diet of negative critiques
Connecting integrating ideas	Seeing ideas as separate and unconnected

Connective conversations build mini-networks that in turn, link to other networks that exponentially enhance the capacity of the community. Michael Fullan's description of this phenomenon bears repeating again, here:

> The power of collective capacity is that it enables ordinary people to accomplish extraordinary things—for two reasons. One is that knowledge about effective practice becomes more widely available and accessible on a daily basis. The second reason is more powerful still—working together generates commitment. Moral purpose, when it stares you in the face through students and your peers working together to make lives and society better, is palpable, indeed virtually irresistible. The collective motivational well seems bottomless. The speed of effective change increases exponentially. (2010, p. 72)

It is equally important that these conversations cut across traditional boundaries. Hallways, departments, grade levels, and school buildings often mark off these traditional boundaries. In Walter Isaacson's biography of Steve Jobs, the late CEO of Apple and Pixar, Isaacson noted that Jobs designed the Pixar building with a central atrium so that all employees would need to run into each other throughout the day. The lobby included the mailboxes, and the meeting rooms and most bathrooms were in the center of the building. According to Jobs, "Everybody has to run into each other" (Isaacson, 2011).

While school leaders might never design a school with one central core, there are architectural lessons to be learned from businesses and schools that built facilities with common spaces (for example: large, interdisciplinary office spaces; meeting rooms near multiple departments; and a well-furnished and inviting faculty dining room). Creating spaces that increase the frequency of unplanned meetings will lead to more conversations, collaboration, and new ideas to improve the school.

Using Feedback Processes to Increase Capacity

Feedback is a powerful means to increase student learning. John Hattie, in one of the largest meta-analyses of education ever conducted, found that feedback has a 0.73 effect size on student learning (2009, p. 162). An effect size of zero means the intervention had no impact on student learning. An effect size of 1.0 indicates an increase of one standard deviation of student achievement or a 50% improvement in the rate of learning. An increase of one standard deviation is equivalent to advancing children's learning by two to three years (2009). To put a 0.73 effect size in perspective with other forms of intervention, "the effect of reducing class size from 25–30 students to 15–20 students is 0.22" (2012, p. 11).

As important as receiving feedback is to student learning, Hattie and Timperley stated that what is needed is quality feedback and where quality feedback has the greatest effect is when teachers receive more and better feedback about their own teaching (2007). Hattie adds that "feedback is more effective when it provides information on correct rather than incorrect responses, and when it builds on changes from previous trials" (2009, p. 175).

Unfortunately, feedback is often given ineffectively, received poorly, or both. Perkins notes that when feedback is critical, it frequently can have a negative effect on relationships. When feedback is conciliatory, it feels better, but has no impact on learning. Perkins offers an alternative form of feedback— *communicative feedback*. This approach combines honest descriptions of behavior with sensitivity toward maintaining relationships. Communicative feedback pays attention to positive aspects of behavior, seeks clarity, asks questions, and raises concerns. It is a balanced form of feedback that is presented in a manner that indicates to the receiver that the observer does not necessarily have all the information and has a growth mindset.

Striking this kind of balance in feedback is neither easy nor straightforward. Part of the reason for this difficulty is that there are tacit rules that govern how feedback is given and received. One cannot be naïve about these norms. For example, people in supervisory roles are assumed to have the authority to give feedback to subordinates. However, when uninvited feedback is given from a subordinate to a boss, the feedback may be hard to deliver or not be welcomed. In addition, rules that govern feedback given to and from peers and coworkers are different. According to Perkins,

> Mostly, they carry expectations for conciliatory feedback. As a friend or colleague, you are supposed to be supportive. Giving uninvited critical feedback is symbolic conduct that offensively

suggests an authority relationship. However, critical feedback is appropriate if it's necessary to save a friend or colleague from a serious gaffe. (2003, p. 63)

Learning systems must change the rules that influence feedback delivery. People who have authority roles in learning school systems, for example, need to seek out and even welcome critical feedback from those who have less authority. Colleagues must become accustomed to delivering more specific and detailed feedback, including suggestions for improvement. These are not easy changes to accomplish within a culture. According to Perkins, "It's a balancing act. When we move forward to offer feedback, we walk through a minefield of social rules and risk setting one off with every step" (p. 63). While this is a challenging prospect, it is one that must be addressed head on. If feedback is blocked, critical information will not be exchanged, and learning will be arrested.

We believe that one of the most significant obstacles to ongoing learning in a school community is the inability to provide specific and honest feedback to educators. As noted earlier, implicit social rules that govern relationships often make that exchange problematic. Educators often feel like they must choose between preserving relationships and providing honest feedback. Many believe that it is not possible to do both.

It is our contention, based on direct experience, that it is possible to preserve relationships and provide honest feedback. However, doing both requires a set of skills on the part of the deliverer of feedback in addition to a significant shift in culture so that all members of the community expect to both share and receive feedback aimed at improving performance. In recognizing both how vital feedback is to building the collective capacity of the organization and how challenging it can be to have feedback improve performance rather than damage relationships or lower morale, leaders face enormous pressure to succeed. While all constituents play a role in shaping culture, leaders have the lion's share of responsibility in this area. Part of the skill set required to communicate feedback effectively relates to emotional intelligence—the ability to know one's own feelings and to be able to manage those feelings, combined with the ability to know how others are feeling and build professional relationships.

Perkins provides some structural guidance in how to enhance the flow of feedback. He recommends

- Avoiding the "five-brain backlash." When groups or teams exceed four members, managing the voices can become unproductively complicated. Keep working groups small when you can—two, three, or four people. Divide up initiatives so that smaller groups can pursue them.

- Using strong and artful facilitation when there are good reasons for a larger group to convene. Stress often leads members of a community or team to regress and respond in ways that diminish the delivery of feedback.
- Avoiding cognitive and emotional oversimplification. These represent the human habit of reducing complex issues and emotions into simple components that often shift meaning and obfuscate a deep understanding of a problem. Cognitive oversimplification can cause issues to become framed as black and white, leaving out the complexity and conflicting values that are often embedded in difficult challenges. Wrestling with ambiguity, complexity, and how to solve new and unanticipated problems will often lead groups and teams to oversimplify in order to arrive at a quick solution.

While these structural recommendations can remove certain obstacles to the flow of feedback, they cannot substitute for the core skill set needed to deliver feedback in a manner that is honest and respectful of relationships. This expertise requires a laserlike focus on teaching and learning combined with a sophisticated understanding of how emotions play a critical role in how messages are heard. Educators need to understand how important it is to deliver information that is critical in a manner that signals positive regard and a belief that the listener can improve. Teachers face a similar challenge with students. When teachers present critical feedback, they also must send three key messages: "This is important; you can do it; I am not going to give up on you" (Saphier, Haley-Speca, & Gower, 2008, p. 262). Among and between adults, the messages are not all that different.

Feedback that provides an educator with rich data about performance, instructional strategies, and collaborative behaviors is the fuel that will ensure that a learning community becomes increasingly more intelligent and effective. While it is true that there are a number of obstacles that can potentially block that feedback from being delivered clearly or being received nondefensively, this kind of feedback exchange is the mainstay of continual improvement.

Another important form of feedback can be delivered through a district's supervision and evaluation system. However, in too many school districts, the system to provide feedback is not functioning effectively and is merely providing educators with superficial feedback about their performance.

The quality of supervision and evaluation is receiving significant national attention. Changes are being adopted across the country aimed at linking teaching to its impact on student learning, increasing the frequency of supervisor visits, and examining other aspects of teaching and learning beyond classroom observations, curriculum planning, and assessment, including family and community engagement and work with colleagues on teams.

A robust system of supervision and evaluation provides educators with ongoing feedback about the quality of their work and its impact on achievement. This form of feedback is critical to the continuous improvement of a learning school system. One of the major purposes of this kind of supervision and evaluation system is to promote growth. A vigorous system must go far beyond the traditional twice-yearly classroom observation cycle. Feedback can come from walkthroughs, examinations of student work and other artifacts of practice, student surveys, teacher surveys (to be shared with administrators), parent surveys, videotaped lessons, and frequent informal conversations about teaching and learning.

There are five feedback streams that have the potential to enhance capacity. While these are not the only ways that feedback can increase the intelligence of a system, they are critical channels to examine when inspecting the capacity-building potential of a learning community. The first two streams, *wisdom from internal* and *external practitioners*, bring practitioners' insight, knowledge, and skills to bear on challenges and problems. The last three streams, *self-reflection*, *supervision and evaluation*, and *data team analyses*, focus on unmet needs and important areas that require strengthening. Together, these five streams circulate the knowledge and necessary skills that are vital resources in a learning school system.

The five streams described above are illustrated in Figure 5.3.

Figure 5.3

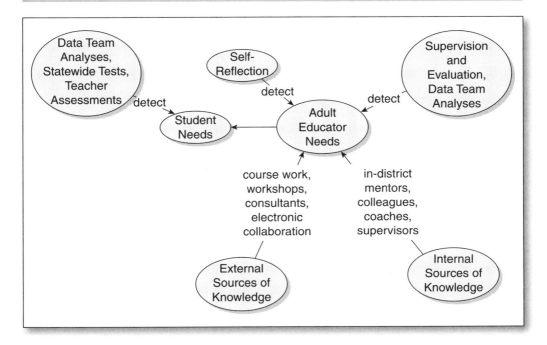

Programs That Are Offered Within the School District

While the needs of school systems will change over time, there are three professional development goals at the center of human capacity building in schools:

1. personal capacity building to improve learning in the classroom;

2. interpersonal capacity building to enable educators to work more effectively in formal teams or fluid groups; and

3. leadership capacity building for all educators (to be discussed in more depth in Chapter 6).

In this section, we will take the reader through a process that will build the three capacities and lead to increased student learning. The model we propose is one way that practitioners can build and lead a program. We recognize there is no one best way to design an effective professional development program.

We start by suggesting that school communities offer some professional development programs at the district level and some at the school level. The districtwide programs should be designed to draw educators from all schools to build both individual and districtwide capacity. At the school level, principals should design their programs to address specific school academic, social, or team goals. In planning these programs, we urge that central office administrators collaborate with principals to ensure that their respective programs, over time, work toward the same overall goals. When school and district goals are divergent, that can lead to frustration and initiative fatigue by teachers and administrators.

At both the district and school level, some programs will be mandatory, some will be suggested to certain faculty members based on interest or teacher evaluations, and most will be voluntary. We have listed below some examples of mandatory, suggested, and voluntary programs.

Mandatory Programs

- District induction programs for all teachers new to the profession.
- District programs for all experienced teachers new to the school district. These programs will differ from the programs for new teachers to the profession in much the same way that we need to differentiate programming for our students.
- District or school programs during the workday when all or most teachers in a school or department need to learn about a new

program to be adopted or expand their knowledge or skills regarding a current program. These programs could be offered during the workday by using substitute teachers or during after-school contract hours such as release days or faculty meeting time.

- School programs organized by principals that are aligned with long-term district goals.

Suggested Programs

- Supervisors encourage teachers to consider professional development programs based on teacher interest or evaluations.

Voluntary Programs

- All other professional development programs offered by the district or school. These programs may focus on content, instructional practice, technology, assessment, or research

In order to ensure that professional development programs are aligned with school and district needs, as judged by highly respected educators, we recommend that school districts establish a K–12 professional development committee. The members of the committee should include both administrators and teachers from all schools and all major departments, including special education. We recommend that a district-level administrator lead the committee, since he or she has access to districtwide resources and has the positional authority to make major decisions.

When the professional development committee is assembled, the committee should survey all educators to determine what programs they say should be offered, examine districtwide data (both standardized and internal data, if available), and survey programs that are offered in the region by educational nonprofit organizations (if any), colleges and universities, and local experts. A survey of external resources may expand the vision of what high-quality programs are available and what teachers need. Sometimes educators within a district may not be aware of new practices outside the school district that could help them.

Once a survey of internal needs and external program possibilities has been completed, we recommend that the professional development committee establish standards for deciding which programs to offer and the course or program learning expectations. The 2005 study of professional development by the Australian government recommends that major professional development initiatives include answers to the following questions (Meiers & Ingvarson, 2005):

- What improvements in student learning outcomes, general or specific, are targeted in the program?
- What are the teaching practices promoted by the professional development program? How might these practices provide better learning opportunities for students?
- What new knowledge and skills are teachers expected to acquire from the professional development activities? How will this knowledge and these skills lead, over time, to changes in teacher practice, and in turn, affect student learning?

Supovitz, a researcher in the area of professional development, suggests that practitioners adopt the following standards when designing professional development (2001, p. 82). Professional development must

1. Show teachers how to connect their work to specific standards for student performance

2. Immerse participants in questioning and experimentation and therefore model inquiry forms of teaching

3. Be intensive and sustained but also dynamic and nimble—much like classroom teaching

4. Include a mix of instructors from within the school system and expert instructors outside the school system when it would benefit teachers (and, by design, student learning) to have opportunities to study, discuss, and implement innovations in educational practice and content with experts in the field

5. Engage teachers in concrete teaching tasks based on teachers' experiences with students

6. Focus on subject matter knowledge and deepen teachers' content skills

7. Be connected to other aspects of school changes

Once short-term programs or full courses have been launched, we recommend that the instructors set the expectation that the knowledge and skills *be used* in the classroom throughout the program or course. Unless educators transfer knowledge and skills into their classrooms, the programs or courses will be of little value to students. To monitor the application of course content, we recommend that instructors assign work to their "students" to ensure the course content is learned, and that they can apply the knowledge and skills in their classrooms, if possible. Instructors should design a process to assess the learning of their "students" throughout the course. For example, we recommend that the instructors conduct precourse inventories, postcourse assessments, and a six-week-out evaluation. During and after the course, we recommend that school leaders encourage colleagues to visit each other's classrooms and share ideas. These visits can help colleagues gain deeper understanding of course content and build trust. If funds are available, we urge districts to hire instructors to provide coaching in the classroom, which will provide both feedback to the learner and ongoing monitoring of the course.

Our final recommendation is to encourage teams of teachers to take the same course. When a group of teachers take the same course, particularly when the teachers regularly work with one another, the group experience is likely to increase ongoing conversations between teachers and motivation to apply course material as well as to deepen understanding and increase student learning.

Based on our own experiences, we see the following advantages and disadvantages to the new model of professional development we propose.

Advantages

When school and district professional development opportunities are based on what teachers need to know to address student needs, team needs, and leadership needs, then professional development opportunities will

- Be more aligned with both school and district needs
- Increase individual teacher capacity
- Build upon the collective capacity of educators
- Support and refine a common, shared vision among all educators throughout the school and district
- Lead to more teachers sharing knowledge and skills with other teachers engaged in the same learning. As more teachers are engaged in common school or district professional development, more teachers will share knowledge and create opportunities to increase collective capacity. The system changes the culture, which leads to more learning all the time. According to Garet et al., "Activities that are

linked to teachers' other experiences, aligned with other reform efforts, and encourage professional communication among teachers appear to support change in teaching practice, even after the effects of enhanced knowledge and skill are taken into account" (2001, p. 936).

- Increase teacher motivation to take school and district professional development courses, since the courses are designed to help them more effectively perform their job
- Change mindsets. In an open, weblike learning environment, educators become exposed to a world of ideas and new practices that are effective. In closed, traditional systems, educators sometimes do not know or acknowledge there is need or urgency to change
- Foster an environment of inquiry and critical thinking—skills that teachers work to build in their students every day. Therefore, the school itself becomes the laboratory and model for both demonstrating continuous learning and teaching students to do the same
- Increase the quality candidates applying for positions, because great teachers love to learn
- Increase student learning (synergy of collective effort)

Disadvantages

Adopting the proposed model of professional development may

- Increase demands on district resources (funds, time, effort, leadership)
- Increase pressure on staff members to learn and change
- Increase faculty resistance due to initiative fatigue or a feeling of ambiguity about which initiatives are priorities and which are "good to know"
- Increase fear due to faculty risk taking
- Decrease sustained change, if professional development is too varied and not aligned to student needs and district or school priorities
- Increase pressure to block or slow down change

Providing high-quality professional development is hard work and must become a core value of the school district over a long period of time. There are no quick fixes to changing and improving professional practice. As we said earlier, effective professional development must be coherent, consistent, systemic, and sustained.

PROVIDING ADEQUATE FUNDING FOR PROFESSIONAL DEVELOPMENT

Providing adequate funds for professional development has always been a challenge for school leaders. Our view is that the challenge is made worse when school superintendents and school boards, and the communities they serve, view professional development as an "extra" program to be funded, rather than as an essential service. We believe that if superintendents and school boards were to become convinced that quality professional development leads to higher student performance, then the types of programs we described in this chapter would be a priority and would be funded.

A few years ago, one of us (Paul Ash) was talking with his school board chair, who asked what was going to happen when the major grant for professional development ran out. To the board chair's surprise, Dr. Ash said that he would eliminate six positions, if other funds were not identified, in order to fully fund the program. He explained that he would rather have 894 highly educated staff members who were well-trained than 900 staff members without adequate professional development. While no superintendent ever wants to eliminate positions, budgets are ultimately about educational choices and most cuts can, over time, be accomplished through attrition.

As school leaders, you may ask how much is enough to fund a quality professional development program. Not including permanent staff positions, such as literacy, mathematics, or technology specialists, or the cost of contract time for professional development, we recommend that about 0.50% to 0.75% of the entire personnel budget is sufficient to pay all instructors for in-district courses. If the school district reimburses teachers for graduate courses, then the professional development budget also needs to include the cost of course reimbursements.

Investing in educator professional development improves student learning, particularly when the programs are aligned with school and district goals, are ongoing, and are embedded in the daily life of the school. In 1996, Greenwald, Hedges, and Laine examined the impact of investments in schools. They researched the relative increase in student learning for every $500 spent (p. 379). The chart that follows shows the relative impact as measured in standard deviation units, for four strategies:

Lowering pupil-teacher ratios	0.04
Increasing teacher salaries	0.16
Increasing teacher experience	0.18
Increasing teacher education	0.22

Their studies show that increasing teacher education had more than five times the impact on learning than lowering class size, which is contrary to common knowledge and public opinion. It is our view that even if the impact on student learning is not fivefold, there is substantial evidence that investing in quality educator learning increases the school system's capacity to educate all students at higher levels.

All of the approaches we have discussed in this chapter focus on increasing educator capacity for current employees. The final section of the chapter discusses how to use the hiring process to increase school and district capacity.

USING THE HIRING PROCESS TO INCREASE CAPACITY

Hiring the right people to join a school system (and supporting them through their first few years of professional practice) is arguably the most important responsibility of a school leader. The challenge is selecting the person from a pool of candidates whose knowledge, skills, dispositions, and attitudes are the best match for the particular job and the best match for the school at large.

Between the two of us, we have interviewed thousands of teacher candidates and hired over 1,000 teachers in our careers. We have learned that the overall selection process is really comprised of three separate but concurrent processes. First, the school leader is hiring a person who has the generic skills to perform the job in any school system. The school leader's job is to ensure that the teacher has outstanding academic credentials and experiences, as verified by transcripts, references, licensure, and interviews. The second process is to determine if the candidate is the best match for the particular job that needs to be filled. Since no candidate is a perfect match for every job, the school leaders must weigh the strengths and weaknesses of each finalist candidate for the actual work required in a particular school, including a record of intellectual curiosity within one's area of expertise and outside of it. Sometimes, school leaders will hire a rookie because the team of teachers can absorb a novice and a young teacher will bring needed diversity to the team. Other times, a seasoned veteran is needed to fill a singleton position (for example, the only physics teacher) or a team needs someone with particular knowledge or skills at the time of hire. The third process is hiring someone who will bring particular strengths or diversity that are needed to build capacity within a department or the entire school.

Each new hire can have a huge impact on a school, either positive or negative. Gathering as much information as possible about each serious candidate is worth every minute. Whether a teacher, support staff member, or administrator is being hired, each hire is an opportunity to fill a job with a highly competent person and can add capacity to an existing team, a school, or the overall school system.

A Checklist of Questions to Pose in Order to Examine the Potential for Capacity Building Within a District
1. To what degree do educators, both administrators and teachers, demonstrate a growth mindset in the face of obstacles and setbacks?
2. How well does the culture embody respect for all individuals and open and honest communication?
3. How well does the district build personal and interpersonal capacity?
4. How well do educators embrace self-reflection? Is it part of both a formal and informal process? Is it part of the supervision and evaluation system?
5. How robust is the feedback that people receive through supervision and evaluation? From colleague to colleague?
6. How would you characterize the degree to which conversations within the district are focused on teaching and learning?
7. To what degree does the district align its professional development programs to school and district needs?
8. To what degree are frontline teachers surveyed about what they believe to be the needs of the district relative to their direct work with students from day to day?
9. To what degree do school leaders create a culture that encourages unplanned discussions and colleague-to-colleague feedback that can lead to creative problem solving and innovation?
10. How strong is the flow of knowledge from outside the system to members within the district? How strong is the flow of practitioner knowledge (from within the district) to other members of the staff?

6 Leaders at All Levels

It is no longer sufficient to have one person learning for the organization, a Ford or a Gates. It's just not possible any longer to figure it out from the top, and have everyone else following the order of the "grand strategist." The organizations that will truly excel in the future will be the organizations that discover how to tap people's commitment and capacity to learn at all levels of the organization.

—Peter Senge (2006)

In chapter 1, we began by asking why very few well-funded school districts have been able to close racial and socioeconomic student achievement gaps. After discussing possible reasons, we stated that the typical K–12 organization, as it is currently designed, has reached the limits of its capacity and needs to be changed to ensure more students achieve at high levels. We can no longer assume that asking educators to work harder, or simply adding some new published program, will significantly increase the quality of teaching and learning in a school system. We believe that in order to raise achievement for all students, schools must be transformed from cultures of teacher autonomy, isolation, and overstandardization, with little professional development, into learning organizations.

In Chapters 3 through 5, we proposed three high-leverage drivers that will enhance teaching and learning and enable educators to break the historical limitations that have held back school capacity. The three drivers are: trust, collaboration in all directions, and capacity building. Since these drivers are attributes of a learning organization, they can only be implemented by a wide array of educators who are committed to a capacity-building culture based on trust and collaboration. In this chapter, we will focus on the fourth driver, leadership at all levels. We will discuss the qualities of school leaders who energize others to expand the school's capacity to educate all students at higher levels. In a K–12 learning organization, the definition of school leader is expanded to include both traditional school leaders and teacher-leaders who take charge and improve learning for themselves and others every day.

PERSONAL QUALITIES OF SCHOOL LEADERS IN A LEARNING ORGANIZATION

The study of leadership is a huge topic, including management, planning, and finance, most of which lies beyond the scope of this chapter. Rather, we focus our attention on one aspect of leadership—the skill set of school leaders in K–12 learning organizations. These leaders are *learning leaders* who promote trust, collaboration, and capacity building, and who build leadership capacity by supporting existing leaders and nurturing new ones throughout the school or school system.

In the sections that follow we describe six skill sets of learning leaders. They are leaders who

1. act on their core values;

2. inspire confidence;

3. build an inclusive network;

4. build a positive school culture;

5. demonstrate sincere inquiry; and

6. support risk taking.

Acts on Core Values

Core values are the fundamental principles that guide an organization's conduct. A school system's core values define what the system stands for and how educators should act every day. When school leaders act every day in a manner that is consistent with their school's core values, they affect their schools far beyond annual goals and strategic plans. When the leader's daily behavior matches his or her espoused values, faculty members are far more likely to believe in the leader and follow the school's goals with enthusiasm.

While it is not unusual for districts to have core values listed in their official publications, it is less common that these values are utilized to drive decisions about student conduct or instruction. When school leaders draw on core values of safety and respect to determine the best approach to a student disciplinary matter, they increase the likelihood that an opportunity for learning and growth will emerge from the incident. Consistent values enable learning school systems to stay on course when battered by a multitude of challenging problems, both internal and external.

When leaders act based on a set of consistent values, they bring authenticity to their work. And while not everyone will agree with every decision, over time members of the community will develop respect for the authentic leader. Without clear, consistent core values and leaders who strongly commit to them, a school or school system may be pulled away from its mission by community pressure or internal politics.

Inspires Confidence

When a doctor, lawyer, or a principal makes a recommendation, why do most people follow the advice? Even though few people are experts in any given field, most people will follow the advice when they have confidence in the person giving the advice. Rosabeth Moss Kanter, who has written extensively about leaders of Fortune 100 companies and managers of sports teams, defines confidence as "positive expectations for favorable outcomes" (2004, p. 7). Just as with medical and legal advice, confidence influences a person's willingness to follow advice from school leaders.

In Chapter 1 we discussed the adverse impact on student learning that can result if teachers hold a limiting view on student intelligence. When teachers believe that certain students cannot learn, or learn as well as others, the teachers' lack of confidence in their students will probably result in lower student effort and performance. In contrast, when educators hold a more liberating view about student capacity, or growth mindset, and believe in their students' abilities to learn at much higher levels, students will gain confidence in themselves, work harder, and learn more.

We believe in the power of positive growth mindsets, and that they are important for all administrators. For example, if principals genuinely believe in their teachers, the teachers are likely to engage in reform activities with commitment. However, if principals do not have confidence in their teachers, the teachers will probably comply with the requests, but are unlikely to put in extra effort to ensure success.

Sustained confidence in a leader is based on long-term success. In a school, a sport team, or any organization, people develop confidence in leaders whom they trust and who demonstrate that following their leadership will yield success. When confidence is built on real success, people feel energized and valued, which leads to more hard work and more success. When schools or companies are successful, they attract talented applicants who want to be part of the winning team, which then builds even more organizational capacity and more success. Conversely, when schools or organizations are failing, workers mistrust their leaders, feel abandoned, and may lose faith that their hard work will make any difference. This lack of confidence may also affect the school or organization's ability to hire talented workers, which may further reduce the school or organization's effectiveness.

We urge school leaders of all schools, whether successful or not, to come to work each day with positive expectations, to show sincere appreciation for hard work, and to acknowledge the learning accomplishments (even small ones) of the staff. Planning for and creating small wins builds confidence that hard work will produce results over time (Kotter, 1996). We expect these behaviors of our teachers toward their students. Leaders who model these behaviors not only support their staff members but also illustrate the expectations that best serve students. Additionally, everyone likes to be recognized and validated for what he or she has accomplished, and positive feelings are contagious. Change often begins with the heart.

Builds an Inclusive Network

In a learning organization, good ideas can come from anywhere. Therefore, it is vital that in a learning school system, school leaders establish inclusive networks of professionals within each school, between the schools, with the central office, and with the outside world. When the leader is connected with a wide array of people, then promising, creative ideas are more likely to get the leader's attention and to be supported. If teachers feel connected to and supported by their leaders, they will be more likely to experiment and try new educational approaches, increasing the creativity and innovation of the school.

Inclusive networks not only help increase educator creativity, they also help build relationships and foster trust between educators, and are vital to the school leaders' ability to make sound, thoughtful educational decisions. It is important that leaders include as many people as they can in key decisions, including people who disagree with them or who may offer pushback. Leaders who reach out in this way, solicit honest feedback, and demonstrate authentic and respectful listening skills are more likely to maintain the trust and support of their teachers and to arrive at better solutions to complex educational problems.

In many ailing school cultures, certain members of the staff are seen as "enemies" or not worthy of attention because of their critical views. Certain members of the school community may become marginalized and even oppose the district's mission. Ironically, the marginalized members of the community may be aware of reasons that the leader's ideas will not work, or work effectively, but their voices are not being heard. For this reason, it is critically important for leaders to understand all perspectives, including ones that might be critical of the current direction of the system.

Builds a Positive School Culture

Haim Ginott, a teacher, child psychologist, and author of the book, *Teacher and Child: A Book for Parents and Teachers,* writes:

> I've come to a frightening conclusion that I am the decisive element in the classroom. It is my personal approach that creates the climate. It's my daily mood that makes the weather. As a teacher I have tremendous power to make a child's life miserable or joyous. I can be a tool of torture or an instrument of inspiration. I can humiliate or humor, hurt or heal. In all situations, it is my response that decides whether a crisis will be escalated or deescalated and a child humanized or dehumanized. (1976, p. 13)

This quote eloquently captures the power and potential that educators have to create a climate or culture within their classrooms—a climate that affects children in much the same way that a sunny day can brighten our outlook or a storm can scare us. Parents of school-age children understand this notion intuitively. They attend an open house, converse with a teacher, and listen carefully to the comments of other parents. These experiences provide an impression of the kind of atmosphere to which their children are exposed within a classroom. How a teacher responds to mistakes, the tone of voice employed when engaging students, and the approach used in communicating expectations are indicators of climate established within a particular teacher's domain.

While a great deal has been written about the strategies that teachers can utilize to craft a responsive and thriving climate or classroom culture, most practitioners know less about the ways this climate can be established by educational leaders within their spheres of influence. Yet developing a vibrant and thriving work climate is an important responsibility of leadership and an essential factor in a learning school system. A school is a system and part of a larger school system. The learning environment in a particular classroom is often influenced by the more encompassing climate or culture that has been established within a department, a school, or even an entire district.

John D'Auria and Matt King have altered the original Ginott quote to describe this aspect of leadership:

> We've come to the conclusion that a leader is the decisive element in the school community. It is the personal approach of that leader which creates the climate. It's the emotional responses of the leader that make the weather. The leader has tremendous power to make the life of teachers and students miserable or joyous. The leader can be a tool of torture or an instrument of inspiration. He or she can humiliate or humor, hurt or heal. In all situations, it is the reactions of the leader that decide whether a crisis will be escalated or deescalated and a community strengthened or diminished. (D'Auria, 2010, p. 8)

One of the most important lessons that we have learned as educators is that a leader's effectiveness is dependent upon his or her ability to create an atmosphere that brings out the best in people and encourages team members to continually improve. Roland Barth writes,

> Unless teachers and administrators act to change the culture of a school, all "innovations," high standards, and high-stakes tests will have to fit in and around existing elements of the culture. They will remain superficial window dressing incapable of making much of a difference. (2002, p. 6)

A major responsibility of school leaders is to nurture and strengthen a school's culture in order to more effectively meet the needs of the children. A school's culture is the lynchpin that connects all the other essential components we have described earlier: developing trust, encouraging collaboration, and building the capacity of the staff. Effective leaders unleash the power of these community-building forces by positively shaping the culture where people work.

Demonstrates Sincere Inquiry

In order to activate power of inquiry, leaders must be skilled in the art of difficult conversations, and must be able to do what former Harvard professor Chris Argyris describes as "combining advocacy with inquiry"(Argyris, Putnam, & Smith, 1985). Too often, leaders find themselves defending their positions against critics, rather than inquiring about how others interpret a problem and its solution. When leaders do not balance their advocacy for ideas with curiosity for how others view the issue, learning is inhibited.

One of the authors first learned about combining advocacy and inquiry at the 2002 annual conference of the National Staff Development Council (NSDC) in Boston. At one conference session, the speaker, Dennis Sparks, who was then the NSDC's executive director, began the session by talking about why leaders must be willing to first share their ideas with faculty members, and then ask them to debate or challenge the ideas. He described three typical approaches used by leaders, and why the third scenario would likely produce the best decisions, faculty learning, and faculty commitment.

1. **The leader advocates for his or her ideas, but does not invite feedback**—In the first scenario, the leader starts the meeting, tells the faculty members his or her view on a new initiative, and *does not* invite comment. A variation of this approach occurs when the leader asks for comments, and faculty members know, based on experience, they are not safe to debate the leader's ideas. In this situation, there is no real exchange of ideas, no possible way to improve the leader's initiative, and little or no learning.

2. **The leader does not advocate for his or her ideas, and asks faculty members what to do**—In the second scenario, the leader starts the meeting by stating a problem, asks the faculty members what they think about the given topic, and never presents his or her ideas. In this type of meeting, faculty members are left wondering what the leader thinks (for example, that he or she lacks courage to share ideas, is withholding ideas, or may not know what to do). This approach may diminish faculty member confidence and trust in the school leader.

3. **The leader both advocates for his or her ideas and authentically seeks out feedback**—In the third scenario, the leader starts the meeting by letting the faculty members know that he or she *really* wants their input and wants them to discuss and debate the ideas presented. The leader tells them that he or she will first share his or her ideas and then will provide time for faculty members to discuss and debate the ideas. In this example, or a variation that includes both genuine advocacy and inquiry, the administrator (or teacher-leader) shows leadership by putting forward his or his ideas, shows openness by allowing the ideas to be discussed and challenged (which builds trust), and shows respect for the faculty members' views by careful listening. This process of advocacy and inquiry permits everyone to engage in meaningful dialogue and build on the leader's ideas or even to reject the ideas. Curiosity about the perspectives of others helps build positive and productive relationships. Genuine inquiry communicates esteem for the thinking of others. Most importantly, inquiry produces new perspectives and knowledge.

Some may argue that the second scenario is the only way to provide an authentic grassroots development of ideas. We believe that with the crowded agendas found in most schools today, when the leader provides a prompt or starting point for thinking and authentically invites others to revise, adapt, or add on to those ideas and seeks out alternative perspectives, it creates an efficient way to build collaboration and manage the scarcity of time.

Supports Risk Taking

In order to break through the current limitations of schools, the educators need to promote a constant flow of new ideas and inventive thinking. Effective school leaders in a learning organization must encourage and validate creative problem solving and support educators who try out new ideas and take risks. Existing problems cannot be solved without new ideas. It is unrealistic to expect that many teachers will analyze current school or classroom practices and recommend new approaches without support from school leaders. Educators who receive support and encouragement are more likely to analyze student performance data and current educational practices and take risks to improve the quality of teaching and learning for students. Schools must also become laboratories for new knowledge. Teachers need to use their classrooms as laboratories to examine student learning and to develop more effective interventions. According to Hattie,

> School leaders and teachers need to create schools, staffrooms, and classroom environments in which error is welcomed as a learning opportunity, in which discarding incorrect knowledge and understanding is welcomed, and in which teachers can feel safe to learn, re-learn, and explore knowledge and understanding. (2012, p. 9)

Currently, schools are highly dependent on research conducted at universities, and school leaders are often hesitant to implement new educational practices that do not yet have validation from studies conducted at universities and other research institutions. While research conducted at universities and other institutions may be statistically reliable, these studies take many years to accomplish and require large sample sizes. Additionally, these research studies may not be narrowly tailored to the needs of an individual school or school district. Consequently, we encourage school leaders to use their own schools and school districts as minilaboratories to determine which practices will work best for their students; the combination of university research with practitioner insights will create the richest and most robust range of solutions to the school or district's educational challenges.

We will now shift our discussion from the qualities of effective leaders in a learning organization to a discussion of why schools need leaders at every level, how to create them, and how to support all leaders, current and new.

BUILDING AND STRENGTHENING LEADERS EVERYWHERE—CENTRAL OFFICE, PRINCIPALS, DEPARTMENT HEADS, AND TEACHERS

In the traditional school system, there are central office leaders such as superintendents and district administrators, middle management leaders such as principals and department heads, and some teacher-leaders. Teacher-leaders may serve as mentors to other teachers or as members of a curriculum committee. In these school systems, classroom teachers are not considered part of the leadership structure, and leadership is often top down. In a K–12 learning organization, however, all faculty members and support staff are encouraged to take on leadership roles, either formally in a part-time position beyond their regular duties or informally, without a title, on an as-needed basis with peer colleagues.

Peter Senge, who was the founding chair of MIT's Society for Organizational Learning, advocates that learning organizations support leadership at every level of an organization—by officially appointed leaders and those who act as leaders, regardless of their title (1996). Senge, who has intensively studied both corporations and public schools, argues that we should abandon the notion that only top management can cause significant change. Organizations need leaders everywhere to invent new ways of improving performance and advocating for changes that are needed. Kouzes and Posner, who served as professors of leadership at Santa Clara University, reached the same conclusion:

> In the thousands of cases we've studied, we've yet to encounter a single example of extraordinary achievement that did not involve the active participation and support of many people. We've yet to find a single instance in which one talented person—leader or individual contributor—accounted for most, let alone 100 percent, of the success. Throughout the years, leaders from all professions, from all economic sectors, and from all around the globe continue to tell us, "You can't do it alone." Leadership is not a solo act; it's a team performance. . . . The winning strategies will be based upon the "we" not "I" philosophy. Collaboration is a social imperative. Without it people can't get extraordinary things done in organizations. (2003, p. 22)

A second major problem with a traditional framework for leadership is compliance. According to Senge, "When genuine commitment is needed, hierarchical authority becomes problematic. . . . No one can force another person to learn if the learning involves deep changes in beliefs and attitudes and fundamental new ways of thinking and acting" (1996, p. 64). In a learning organization, everyone can contribute and advocate change. Everyone can provide leadership within his or her work group to implement the new plan.

In Chapter 8, we will discuss how great ideas can diffuse from a few individuals to an entire school system. We will discuss how the diffusion of new ideas, programs, and innovations requires local leaders (teachers and middle managers) who will advocate change, and executive leaders who have the authority and resources to support significant change throughout a school or school system.

DEVELOPING NEW LEADERS

According to a study conducted by the National Association of Secondary Principals, a dedicated and dynamic principal is a key attribute of a high performing school (2004, June 9). Unfortunately, the Wallace Foundation reported that while "there are plenty of 'certified' applicants . . . there seems to be a dearth of candidates with high-level leadership skills. . . . Superintendents continue to express dissatisfaction about adequate leadership of new principals." (Roza, 2003). Additionally, in 2006 the Pennsylvania Association of Elementary and Secondary School Principals published a study of nine states from Pennsylvania to Maine that found that over 42% of principals and assistant principals said that they will retire from their positions within the next five years.

In our judgment, based on decades of hiring principals, there is a principal shortage in the United States that must be addressed. Losing a principal or any school leader can have a major impact on a school. When an effective principal or other school leader retires or resigns, he or she leaves behind years of working relationships with colleagues and district knowledge. The new hire, no matter how competent, will need to establish relationships with numerous educators, students, and parents; to build trust; to learn about programs; and to gain a deep understanding of school and community values. When a school leader retires or resigns, forward momentum on current initiatives may be temporarily slowed or be lost permanently.

In 2009, McKinsey and Company published a study of 20 systems and 200 system leaders from all over the world to determine the factors that contributed to their students' success. The researchers found that one of the major factors related to high student performance was *continuity of the system's leadership*. This report went on to emphasize the importance of generating a system of leadership from within the district in order to ensure "that there is a continuity of purpose and vision in sustaining the system's pedagogy and improvement" (Mourshed, Chijioke, & Barber, 2010, p. 22).

Given that hiring an outstanding principal is difficult and the change in personnel may affect a school's capacity to function at a high level, we recommend that school districts implement a plan to develop new leaders. By nurturing new and talented leaders from within the district, not only can a school system expand the pool of quality applicants for future jobs; in addition, the newly trained leaders may be more likely to stay in the district and become part of the team finding new educational solutions.

In order to build future leadership capacity, we recommend that school systems offer leadership courses and experiences as part of the district's professional development program. Ideally, the program should be designed for the three types of school leaders: current administrators, future school administrators, and teachers who want to become teacher-leaders without leaving the classroom. The first two programs would need to be adaptable based on what skills or knowledge are pertinent for current leaders or required for licensure. For example, current leaders may need to expand their supervision and evaluation skills or take a course on how to have difficult conversations with supervisees. Educators seeking an administrator license may need to work in the district to complete an internship. The third program, for teacher-leaders, is a relatively new concept in public schools today. In 2011, the National Education Association, 19 national organizations, 11 state agencies, and 8 institutions of higher education published teacher-leader model standards.[1] According to the National Board for Professional Teaching Standards, teacher-leaders are defined as teachers who, "working with principals, are instructional and organizational change agents who have a critical impact on school, teacher, and student success" (2012).

We see the same six leadership qualities that we discussed at the beginning of the chapter exhibited by the teacher-leaders. Teacher-leaders, department leaders, principal leaders, and central administration leaders all act on their core values, inspire confidence, build an inclusive network, build a

[1]The standards were developed by the Teacher Leadership Exploratory Consortium (comprised of a broad array of education organizations, state education agencies, teacher leaders, principals, superintendents, and institutions of higher education). The complete description of each standard can be found at http://www.nbpts.org/products_and_services/national_board_certifica1

positive culture, demonstrate sincere inquiry, and support risk taking. These are the same six skills that promote a culture of trust, collaboration, and capacity building in the classroom to the school board room.

In a learning organization, everyone can find his or her passion to improve student learning. Some educators will choose formal leadership positions, while others may choose to lead their teacher team or lead a district committee. Expanding leadership development is one way that districts can expand their capacity to bring teams of educators together to solve complex educational problems.

LEADERSHIP THAT CONNECTS THE HEART AND MIND

While much has been written about the important skills that educational leaders need to be effective instructional leaders, excellent managers, and skillful communicators, there have been far fewer descriptors of the personal and social behaviors of leaders that contribute to a thriving culture. One notable exception is the leadership matrix developed by the NYC Leadership Academy. NYC Leadership Academy created their Leadership Performance Standards Matrix from extensive research that examined behaviors linked to leaders who create positive change in student achievement. While the complete Leadership Matrix contains traditional standards related to student achievement, parent outreach, and instructional expertise, it also contains standards for the personal and interpersonal behaviors of effective leaders. The following excerpt from the matrix contains a sample of the latter, including indicators of those standards and examples of behaviors that would meet that standard.

Leadership Dimension	Meeting the Standard
1.0 Personal Behavior	
1.1 Reflects an appropriate response to situations	Leader considers the consequence of his or her actions, anticipates possible responses or reactions, and accurately adjusts behavior accordingly.
	Leader understands and manages emotions and is aware of their impact.
1.2 Consistent with expressed belief system and reflect personal integrity	Leader's behavior reflects core values at all times.
	Leader's actions are transparent and there are no surprises.

Leadership Dimension	Meeting the Standard
1.4 Values different points of view within the organization	Leader actively seeks and makes use of diverse and controversial views. Leader welcomes and appreciates diversity in demonstrable ways.
2.0 Resilience	
2.1 Reacts constructively to disappointment, admits errors, and learns from mistakes and setbacks	Leader quickly transitions from emotional to strategic responses to mistakes and setbacks.
2.3 Handles disagreement and dissent constructively	Leader transforms disagreement and dissent into opportunities.
3.0 Communication	
3.6 Communication reflects careful analysis and the ability to listen	Leader attends and responds to subtle nonverbal cues in others. Leader deals with difficult issues honestly and directly, uses low-inference data and provides examples. Leader actively pursues disconfirming evidence for conclusions drawn.
6.0 Learning	
6.2 Understands the role of a learner	Leader is able to identify and take ownership of professional and leadership development needs. Leader understands that the best ideas emerge and are acted upon regardless of the source. Leader values mistakes in the service of learning and moves from the known to the unknown. Leader uses feedback and self-reflection to enhance own learning.
9.0 Leadership Development	
9.1 Develops leadership in others	Leader provides formal and informal leadership opportunities for others and encourages them to exercise appropriate authority in those areas for which they are held accountable.
10.0 Climate and Culture	
10.1 Motivates and encourages others to achieve strategic goals	Leader models, encourages, and reinforces efficacy in individuals to produce results and persevere even when internal and external difficulties interfere with the achievement of strategic goals. Leader generates a sense of urgency by aligning the energy of others in pursuit of strategic priorities.

While we have understood for a while the important responsibilities that leaders have for student learning, we are just beginning to understand how effective leaders support the learning of the adults within a school community. It is the ongoing learning of the adults that ensures that the system continually improves. It is for this reason that we believe that it is the quality of leadership within a district and its ability to support "leadership everywhere" that is one of the key determinants of whether or not the system will *break through* the limitations that restrain its capacity.

TEN QUESTIONS TO EXAMINE THE STATE OF LEADERSHIP WITHIN A DISTRICT

1. How well does the climate support continuous learning?

2. How well do leaders create an inclusive environment for all educators?

3. How well do leaders inspire confidence?

4. How well do leaders balance advocacy with inquiry? Do they support risk taking?

5. To what degree does leadership depend on collaborative relationships as opposed to positional authority to achieve system goals?

6. How apparent are the core values of the system in daily interactions?

7. How clear is the system's vision to all stakeholders?

8. What is the level of collective responsibility for achieving that vision?

9. To what degree does the district provide leadership with professional development?

10. Does the district's evaluation criteria include an assessment of the leader's personal behaviors, including resiliency, communication skills, use of feedback, and attention to school culture?

7 Why Building a K–12 Learning School System Is So Difficult

There is nothing more difficult to plan, more doubtful of success, nor more dangerous to manage than the creation of a new order of things. . . . Whenever his enemies have the ability to attack the innovator they do so with the passion of partisans, while the others defend him sluggishly, so that the innovator and his party alike are vulnerable.

—Niccolo Machiavelli, *The Prince*

Leading a school or school district is very hard work. The work is intellectually and emotionally demanding, the work hours are very long, there are no "cookbooks" on how to produce excellent instruction, and rarely are school leaders ever thanked for leading instructional change. The harsh reality is that an effective school leader lives in a world of high aspirations, unmet student needs, insufficient resources, a lack of understanding by staff members and parents, and pressure from multiple constituencies whenever the school leader tries to make major instructional improvements or personnel changes. The job can be very lonely and frightening, particularly when school leaders decide they must make tough decisions that will upset some constituency (parents, teachers, students, unions, school board members, or supervisors).

The purpose of Chapters 1 through 6 was to show the historical limitations of most school systems and then introduce the four internal systemic drivers that will contribute to breaking the limitations of the past and unleashing a dynamic K–12 learning school system. If we had wanted to paint a Pollyanna picture of a K–12 learning school system, we would have ended the book after Chapter 6 on this upbeat note. However, in the real world, leading change is extremely difficult and will challenge the intellectual and emotional fiber of the best school administrators. In Chapter 7, we discuss why deep systemic change is very difficult to achieve even when the conditions for change are in place. The primary purpose of Chapter 7 is to present the very real obstacles teachers and administrators must overcome if they intend to create a K–12 learning school system. The sheer desire and will to create a collaborative learning culture is not enough.

LEADING CHANGE

Go to any major library and you will find at least a hundred books on leadership in the private sector with prescriptions on how to lead change. For example, in John Kotter's bestseller, *Leading Change,* the Harvard Business School professor describes his eight-step change process for top-down change initiatives in large private organizations (1996). *Business Week* named Kotter as one of the top leadership gurus in America ("Rating," 2001). What you won't find in these libraries are many chapters in any book on why lasting change is unbelievably difficult to accomplish in a school system.

While we deeply respect the ideas by Kotter and others on how to change a company to make it more profitable, changing a school system is about changing the lives of children. In the private sector, the owner of the company or board of directors can measure success by dollars and cents. In a private business, the financial standard for success is clear and unambiguous and can be measured. However, in a public school system, parents and teachers often fight about what we want "our" children to learn and how success should be measured. The history of education is filled with fights over new ways to teach children better (for example, whole language, constructivist mathematics, open classrooms, and the use of standardized tests).

Leading change in public schools will arouse passionate discussions over academic content, values, and pedagogy. Ron Heifetz, in his book *Leadership Without Easy Answers,* describes changing human behavior and attitudes as adaptive work, which arouses passion and resistance. Heifetz argues that adaptive work requires learning and cannot be mandated.

> Adaptive work consists of the learning required to address conflicts in the values people hold, or to diminish the gap between the values people stand for and the reality they face. Adaptive work requires a change in values, beliefs, or behavior. (1994, p. 13)

THE CHANGE PROCESS AS A LEARNING PROCESS

Whether a person is a CEO of a major company or a superintendent of schools, leading change within an organization is a multistage process and not an event. In the chart below, three major experts on organizational change identify the stages of change. Daniel Yankelovich is the founder of the Yankelovich/New York Times Poll and former chairman of the non-partisan group Public Agenda; Gene Hall is the Dean of Education at the University of Nevada; and John Kotter is a former Harvard Business School professor. All three researchers identify the same three major phases: the awareness stage, the resistance stage, and the integration stage (See Figure 7.1).

In all three models, the leader's job during first stage (the awareness stage) is to explain what change is needed and why. During this stage, the leader must present all constituents with a clear picture of the desired

Figure 7.1

	Ash and D'Auria	Yankelovich	Hall	Kotter
Stage 1	Awareness/ Innovation stage	1. Awareness	1. Talking stage	1. Create a sense of urgency
				2. Put together a strong enough team to direct the process
		2. Urgency		3. Create an appropriate vision
				4. Communicate that vision broadly
Stage 2	Learning/ Resistance/ Working-through stage	3. Look for answers	2. Tinkering stage	5. Remove obstacles
		4. Resistance		6. Create short-term wins
		5. "Choicework"		
Stage 3	Integration stage	6. Initial, intellectual acceptance	3. Transforming stage	7. Build momentum and use that momentum to tackle tougher change and problems
		7. Moral acceptance		8. Anchor the new behavior in the organizational culture

(For more information, see Cambron-McCabe, Cunningham, Harvey, and Koff, 2004; Kotter, 1996; and Yankelovich and Friedman, 2011.)

change and, in Yankelovich's and Kotter's models, also create a sense of urgency to motivate others.

During the second stage (the resistance or working-through stage), the leader is likely to encounter serious resistance from stakeholders. Yankelovich calls this the *working-through stage*, rather than resistance stage, since all participants, including the leader, must confront the need for change, consider the pros and cons of the proposed actions, and struggle with trade-offs. According to Yankelovich, "In this stage of the learning curve people struggle to reconcile their positions on issues with their core values. In this sometimes stormy process, emotions play a more prominent role than objective analysis and deliberation" (Yankelovich & Friedman, 2011, p. 18). Leaders can expect backsliding, procrastination, and avoidance by some players. The back-and-forth process includes both a resistance and learning until the leader works through the problems in discussion with others.

During this second stage, the leader has a choice: either to view resistance by stubborn employees, parents, and board members as a "headwind," which must be pushed through or to use this stage as a process in which all participants learn deeply about the proposed change and its goals, work to improve the plan, and take steps to ensure adequate support from all participants. In a K–12 learning school system, successful leaders use the second stage as a learning process that encourages faculty, parents, and board members to ask questions, share ideas, and improve the proposed plan.

In the third stage (the integration stage), stakeholders accept the change, its rationale, and the pros and cons. During this stage, there is intellectual and emotional acceptance, transformation, and anchoring of the change by the stakeholders.

DIFFUSION OF INNOVATION

In the mid-2000s, Everett Rogers's book titled *Diffusion of Innovations* was one of the most cited books in the social sciences (1995). For more than 30 years, Rogers studied the rate at which the public adopted new innovations. His theories have been used to examine how quickly the public adopts new technology, biological innovations, and ideas through communication. While his extensive research did not examine how quickly ideas were adopted in education, his studies in a wide range of fields strongly suggest that there is a pattern to the adoption of new ideas: some people adopt them rapidly, some people are the followers, and some resist change.

Rogers proposed that adopters of any new innovation or idea fall into five categories: innovators (2.5%), early adopters (13.5%), early majority (34%), late majority (34%), and laggards (16%). Rogers acknowledged that a person might be an innovator for one innovation or idea but not for another. Figure 7.2 graphically represents the categories listed above.

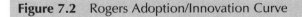

Figure 7.2   Rogers Adoption/Innovation Curve

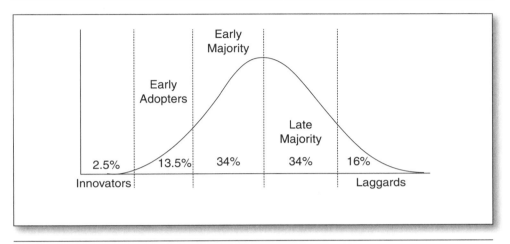

Reprinted with the Permission of Free Press, a Division of Simon & Schuster, Inc. from *Diffusion of Innovations*, Fifth Edition by Everett M. Rogers. Copyright © 1995, 2003 by Everett M. Rogers. Copyright © 1962, 1971, 1983 by The Free Press. All rights reserved.

It is interesting that Rogers found that the adoption process follows a similar learning cycle to that identified by Yankelovich, Hall, and Kotter (awareness, working through, and integration). Rogers identified a five-step diffusion process for organizations (p. 421).

THE MECHANISM OF DIFFUSION

Initiation Phase

1. Agenda Setting—General organizational problems that may create a perceived need for innovation.

2. Matching—Fitting a problem from the organization's agenda with an innovation.

Implementation Phase

3. Refining and restructuring—People engage in activities that lead to a choice to adopt or reject the innovation.

4. Clarifying—The relationship between the organization and the innovation is defined more clearly.

5. Routinizing—The innovation becomes an ongoing element in the organization's activities and loses its identity.

While Rogers chose to combine his five-step process into two major phases (initiation and implementation), his diffusion theory also fits nicely with the three major phases identified by Yankelovich and Hall and the model we have described.

Ash and D'Auria	Rogers
Awareness/Innovation Stage	Agenda Setting
	Matching
Learning/Resistance/Working-Through Stage	Refining/Restructuring
	Clarifying
Integration Stage	Routinizing

According to Rogers's research, about 16% of the general population will quickly embrace new ideas. Who are the other 84% who will resist proposed initiatives and why?

THE RESISTERS: WHO THEY ARE

Are You an Obstacle to Change?—Why Is Change So Hard From the Leader's Point of View?

It is tempting to blame others for resisting change in your school or school system. However, sometimes the first line of resistance is the administrator him- or herself.

We have listed below six of the major factors that may hold you back from leading the change you want. Before launching a significant change in your school or school system, we ask each reader to consider his or her strengths and weaknesses in regard to each factor.

1. Personal Capacity—Do I have the capacity to figure out how to change a system or practice to achieve a desired outcome? Am I willing to do the very hard work?

2. Political Risk—Can I convince enough people to support the change? Who will support the proposed change and who will oppose it?

3. Practicality—Even if I know what change is needed (intellectual), and know we can garner enough internal and external support (political), do I have sufficient resources to succeed (money, time, human capital, energy, and drive)?

4. Personal Risk—What will happen to me if I promote the change (short- and long-term)? If the new initiative is a failure, can I withstand the impact in my work environment?

5. Emotional Impact—Do I have the intestinal fortitude to work for the vision and slog through resistance and severe criticism?

6. Social Impact—Am I willing to weaken long-standing personal and professional relationships and reduce trust in order to actualize the vision?

The good news is that you don't have to affirmatively answer the questions in all six categories during the awareness stage of leading change. During that first part of the change process, you still have the luxury of time to float an idea or initiative to others without significant risk to you. During the awareness stage, you can test the waters to find out: Do people think your idea has merit? How could they improve the idea? How many people agree with the idea? Will they support the change? Are there enough resources to launch the change? Once you have clarified your vision, built a guiding coalition of supporters, explained why the change is needed and why it will produce the intended outcomes, we then urge you to consider the questions in all six categories before finally deciding to push the change. Please see the end of this chapter for the full list of questions per category. Some of these questions may get answered during the awareness stage. Other questions are highly personal and will require the school administrator to reflect deeply about his or her own capacity and drive.

Are Other People the Obstacle to Change?

Yes—It is fact that the superintendent of schools cannot implement most changes in a K–12 school system unilaterally. While the superintendent of a public K–12 district may have some independent powers, most authority, both formal and informal, is distributed among numerous constituencies. That means that, when implementing change, there are many, many other stakeholders in your community who can support, slow down, or stop that planned change.

For example, suppose that after many months of discussions with your principals and teachers, you have decided to announce that all teachers, K through 12, need common planning time each week to support teacher collaboration. However, since you do not have the unilateral authority to implement the changes you want, you most likely will need to seek out agreement from the principals (to support the change), the union (to change the teachers' contracts), the school board (to change the contract), the teachers who will implement the change, the parents (if the change will impact their child's schedule), and town, city, county, or school district officials and residents if additional funding will be needed for professional development or the overall teacher bargaining agreement. Even if outstanding ideas emerge from within the K–12 learning community itself, implementing these ideas will usually require support from multiple constituencies.

To illustrate the minimum number of constituencies in a small school system, we chose a school system in a town with one high school, one middle school, and one elementary school. In this small school system, there are at least fourteen constituencies who could potentially block a good idea if funding is needed. Even if no funding is needed, there are countless subgroups who could exercise power. The fourteen major constituencies are:

1. The School Board
2. The Union
3. The Town's Finance Committee
4. The Town's Board of Selectmen
5. The Town Meeting
6. The High School Principal
7. The High School Faculty
8. The High School Parents
9. The Middle School Principal
10. The Middle School Faculty
11. The Middle School Parents
12. The Elementary School Principal
13. The Elementary School Faculty
14. The Elementary School Parents

The good news is that in most school systems, there is a moderate to high degree of trust among and between the various constituencies. As mentioned earlier, a high level of trust is one of the major drivers that makes it possible for different groups to talk and find ways to change a learning organization. However, in some school systems, particularly urban school systems, one constituency may have the power to block a plan that would improve the schools.

While leading significant change is difficult, we are not aware of research that shows K–12 districts cannot be led systemically. In fact, in a recent unpublished study of all superintendents in Massachusetts, 86% of the superintendents reported that their working relationship with their school committee (board) was highly effective (43%) or somewhat effective (43%). These same superintendents also reported that their "school committee supports me and my actions regularly" (81%), and they "like

the superintendency well enough to encourage a son or daughter showing the aptitude to pursue it" (Strongly agree 24%, and agree 56%). The
Massachusetts study shows that superintendents like their work and feel
supported by their school board.

WHAT ELSE CAN GET IN YOUR WAY?

The Debris Field

As an experienced school administrator, you are highly organized. You
have carefully planned the year. The district annual and school goals, as
well as your requested budget, have been approved; the capital projects
are well underway; and all teachers have been hired for the fall. Then, the
unexpected happens, which throws a major obstacle in your way and
stops your well-planned initiatives. We call these unplanned obstacles *the
debris field*. Although not as dangerous as walking through a minefield,
every experienced administrator has and will encounter unexpected
events (the debris field) that will upset even the most carefully made
plans. Here is one real example from the Boston area.

One day in mid-August of 2010, the superintendent of schools received
a telephone call from the director of public facilities that a recent air test
showed polychlorinated biphenyl (PCB) levels were well above the EPA
safety guidelines in an elementary school. The superintendent and the
facilities director were forced to spend significant funds to remove window caulk that contained PCBs, expecting that the PCB airborne levels
would drop. A week later, just before the students returned in the fall, new
test results showed no change in airborne PCB levels. Removing the window caulk that contained PCBs did not lower PCB levels in the air.

On September 6, during the first week of school, hundreds of angry
parents and residents filled the town's auditorium to hear about the PCB
problem. The superintendent of schools had assembled a panel that
included representatives from an environmental consulting company, a
representative from the Environmental Protection Agency, the chairman of
the local Department of Public Health, the local director of public health,
the director of public facilities, and himself. The local experts and the EPA
stated that exposure to PCBs is not a short-term health concern for children. Based on the experts' opinions, the superintendent recommended
that the school be kept open for now while a PCB mitigation plan was
established and implemented. He indicated that he would establish a PCB
advisory committee that included parents, teachers, local officials, and
expert consultants to advise the administration. However, many, many
parents said their children were in danger and demanded the school be

closed immediately. One parent said that even one molecule of PCB was too much for his child.

Resolving this crisis meant that nearly all other goals for the year were pushed to the back burner, and hundreds of hours of staff time were reallocated to meet with experts, parents, elected officials, union officials, state officials, and educators in the school. Ultimately, reducing the PCB levels below the EPA guidelines cost nearly 1 million dollars.

While this debris field crisis is an extreme case, all administrators will encounter the debris field from time to time: severe union issues, a major budget shortfall due to unexpected special education placements, a tragic event regarding student safety, or parents who rise up to complain about some topic that was not on the radar screen.

Unlike the initiatives you choose to first study and then launch, debris field obstacles come without warning and will probably challenge your very core as a leader. In the PCB scenario, the superintendent had no expertise in environmental science, many parents were hysterical, the science on the safety of PCBs was new, safety questions could not be answered with certainty, some long-term teachers in the school began to ask about possible cancer risks, the school board looked to the superintendent to lead (what did he know?), the EPA expected prompt action, and there were no funds in the school budget to handle the crisis. This crisis challenged all six personal areas of the best administrators: personal capacity, political skills, practical considerations, personal risk, emotional capacity, and social capital (see The Obstacle Course, p. 152).

Too Many Initiatives

Talk to almost any schoolteacher and you are likely to hear that he or she is overworked, with too many demands and not enough resources. Now, in this environment, imagine that the school leader or superintendent suggests that a new initiative be added. Is it any wonder why teachers may resist or seriously question the wisdom and urgency of the new program?

Earlier in this chapter, we described the usual processes for presenting, debating, and implementing a new idea that allows faculty members to discuss program efficacy and alternatives. One other idea we suggest you consider is to hold a "pull the weeds before you plant the flowers" party (Reeves, 2006, pp. 89–90). Ask faculty members to attend a faculty meeting and bring one program they want to discontinue (a "weed") because they believe that program is no longer needed or effective. Reeves suggests three rules to help schools stay focused on what is important.

1. Use intergrade dialogue to find the essentials and eliminate what is not essential.

2. Prune away the small stuff that uses up valuable time.

3. Set the stage for a weed-free garden. Respect teachers' time, and start and end meetings on time.

The Tyranny of *or*

Jim Collins, in the book *Built to Last*, wrote about the successful habits of visionary companies that have been highly successful (2002). One habit he found was that great companies believe in the "Genius of the *and*" and avoided the "Tyranny of *or*." In these visionary companies, he found that there was an "ability to embrace both extremes of a number of dimensions at the same time." Instead of choosing between A or B, they figure out a way to have both A and B. In companies that fell into the trap of the Tyranny of *or*, leaders and regular employees believed you always had to make a choice between two seemingly different ideas. In Collins's book, he identified the following choices (p. 43):

- You can have change *or* stability
- You can be conservative *or* bold
- You can have low cost *or* high quality
- You can have creative autonomy *or* consistency and control
- You can invest for the future *or* do well in the short term

In education, we too have fallen into these traps:

- Whole language *or* phonics
- Traditional mathematics *or* constructivist mathematics
- Homogeneous grouping of students *or* heterogeneous grouping of students
- Self-contained classrooms *or* flexible grouping of students between classrooms
- Top-down leadership *or* bottom-up leadership
- Teacher autonomy *or* teacher collaboration

One of the obstacles that prevents school leaders from creating a whole school system out of its many parts is falling into the trap of the tyranny of *or*. The more we allow people to create false dichotomies, the more opportunities we lose to offer students diverse choices, create synergy between multiple approaches, and the more we allow people to remain in their silos. In a learning school system, the goal is to create collaboration in all directions and combine programs with different philosophies into one coherent system. For example, we need to both honor the work of the individual teacher in the classroom *and* support opportunities for teachers to collaborate in and outside the classroom. Since none of us are as smart as all of us, we need to find ways to bring together educators who have different ideas, rather than allow only one set of good ideas to survive and push out opportunities for growth. We recommend that learning leaders explicitly talk about the power of *and*, even if it makes some people uncomfortable.

Resisters Don't Share Your Interests and Goals

Anyone who has bought a car knows that the car dealership's interest is to make a sale and maximize profit, while your goal is to buy the car at the lowest price. In this example, perhaps the two sides can reach an agreement by splitting the difference. However, in schools there are some times when the parties cannot split the difference.

In one system, the superintendent wanted to start a Mandarin Chinese program, based on the importance of China today and the fact that there are 800 million Mandarin speakers in China alone. After proposing his new idea, he learned that the middle school French and Spanish teachers opposed the new program. After some discussions with the middle school principal, the superintendent was told that the teachers were worried that a new Mandarin program would mean fewer students taking their subjects and that some veteran teachers might lose their jobs.

Once in a while, the interests of the faculty members may collide with the interests of the students and no compromise is possible. In such cases, if the leader is convinced that students have a compelling need that can only be met by launching the new initiative, then this is the rare case in which the leader must make a decision, explain it clearly to all constituencies, and be prepared for some upset faculty members.

Lack of Trust, Collaboration in All Directions, Leadership Everywhere, and Capacity Building (The Four Drivers of Change)

In Chapters 3 through 6, we described the four major drivers of change needed to significantly improve the quality of a school or school system. We argued that high levels of all four attributes at the same time will create a synergy and unleash teacher potential across the district. On the other hand, if these four drivers are low or absent, then launching any new initiative is likely to fail. Consider what would happen without the four drivers:

1. Lack of Trust—Without trust, why would any faculty member, parent, or school board member follow the school or district leader? Without trust, it is less likely that faculty members will make the leap of faith from the "Present Known" to the "Promised Land."

2. Lack of Collaboration—Without collaboration from colleagues, it is much less likely that faculty members will agree to the new initiative.

3. Lack of Leadership—If the school or district administrator is not respected as a leader, then few faculty members, parents, or board members will ever agree to the plan. Ultimately, people follow leaders because they believe in the vision and believe that the leader can successfully implement the vision.

4. Lack of Capacity Building—Without meaningful capacity-building activities, why would faculty members agree to a new initiative and risk professional failure, or worse, having an adverse impact on students? A lack of support for faculty members will increase resistance to the new idea and cause failure if it is mandated.

In conclusion, we urge the reader to take the Obstacle Course that appears in the next few pages. We have assembled this self-assessment tool so that the reader can quickly assess whether he or she has the tools needed to launch a new initiative and overcome the likely obstacles.

THE OBSTACLE COURSE

A Self-Assessment of What Obstacles Are in Your Way

Yes	Maybe	No
(Not an obstacle)	**?**	**(Is an obstacle)**

Are You an Obstacle to Change?	
Personal Capacity	
	1. Do I believe I have the personal capacity to figure out how to change the system or practice to achieve the desired outcome?
	2. Am I willing to do the very hard work necessary to plan and implement the change?
Political	
	1. Can I convince enough people to support the change?
	2. Do I know who will support the proposed change and who will oppose it?
Practical	
	1. Even if I know what change is needed (intellectual), and know that we can garner enough internal and external support (political), do I have sufficient resources to succeed (money, time, human capital, energy and drive)?
Personal Risk	
	1. Can I predict what will happen to me if I promote the change (short- and long-term)?
	2. If the new initiative is a failure, can I withstand the impact in my work environment?
Emotional	
	1. Do I have the intestinal fortitude to work for the vision and slog through resistance and severe criticism?
Social	
	1. Am I willing to weaken longstanding personal and professional relationships and reduce trust in order to actualize the vision?

Is Your School Board an Obstacle to Change?

1. Does the school board have confidence in your leadership?

2. Do you anticipate that the school board will support your proposed change?

3. Do you already have sufficient resources (money and staff) to implement the change?

Is the Union Leadership an Obstacle to Change?

1. Does the union contract allow you to make the change without the union's support?

2. If you do not legally need the union's support to make the change, will the union support the change?

3. Do you have a cooperative working relationship with the union leadership?

4. If you answered *no* to the prior question, will the school board support changing the teachers' contract during the next round of collective bargaining? (If you answered *yes* or *maybe* to the prior question, then skip this question.)

Are the Principals or the Superintendent an Obstacle to Change?

1. In the past, have the principals, as a group, and the superintendent supported your vision?

2. Are you, the principals, and the superintendent a high-performing team?

3. Are the principals by themselves a high-performing team?

4. Do the principals have the backbone to lead your proposed change?

5. Does the superintendent have the backbone to lead your proposed change?

6. Are most principals and the superintendent willing to have difficult conversations with staff members?

7. Are the principals willing to relinquish some site-based management to be part of a K–12 team?

Are Your Parents an Obstacle to Change?

1. Are your parents pleased with the schools?

2. Will the proposed change have little or no direct effect on the parents or their children?

3. Are your parents comfortable with little or no involvement in decision making?

4. Are you able to make the proposed change without parent support?

(Continued)

(Continued)

Are the Teachers an Obstacle to Change?	
	1. Is the proposed change supported by a compelling educational vision?
	2. Do teachers have the energy to support and implement the proposed change? Are they burdened with too many other initiatives?
	3. Are the teachers likely to support the proposed change?
	4. Are those likely to resist the change well respected?
	5. Do you have the time needed to provide needed dialogue?
	6. Will you have adequate professional development to support the teachers?
	7. Will you have sufficient teacher collaboration to support the change?
	8. Will the proposed change mean an increase of autonomy for teachers?
Are the Local Governing Boards and Officials an Obstacle to Change?	
	1. Does your proposed change require additional funds?
	2. Does your proposed change require a vote of non-school people?
	3. Does your proposed change affect other residents (in addition to parents)?
Are There Other Factors That Are Obstacles to Change?	
	1. The school or school system has the resources to overcome the obstacles listed above?
	2. Can this proposed change be integrated into other initiatives? (genius of *and*, not the tyranny of *or*)
	3. Is the proposed change in the interest of all groups, including the students?
Are Other People or Other Organizations an Obstacle to Change?	
List them here.	

How Strong Are the Four Drivers in Your System?			
	Weak	Moderate	High
Trust			
Collaboration			
Leadership			
Capacity Building			

8

Whole School System Change and the Diffusion of Innovation

In previous chapters we focused on the four lead drivers that increase the collective capacity of a school or school system to improve student learning for all students: increasing trust, collaboration in all directions, capacity building, and having leaders at all levels of the school system. While these drivers are needed to catalyze educational innovation and change, they are not sufficient to overcome likely resistance from multiple constituencies, or to ensure that innovations spread throughout the school or school system at a deep level. In Chapter 7, we discussed some of the obstacles to change in an educational setting. In Chapter 8, we present a school- and districtwide model of educational innovation that builds upon the ideas presented in earlier chapters. The model is designed to help educational leaders support initiatives at the individual or team level, to bring the most promising ideas to the implementation level, and to work through the resistance/learning stage to deep implementation and integration throughout a school system.

The model begins with the assumption that educational leaders must deeply value a culture of trust, collaboration, leadership, and capacity building, and must act on those values. As discussed previously, these conditions will break down teacher isolation and increase the rate at which teachers innovate and share best practices with others in their work groups. However, the production of promising ideas within a work group does not guarantee that the ideas will spread to other teachers in the school or to other schools.

For example, in a school with typical teacher isolation, few best practices or innovative solutions will migrate to other educators; there may be some outstanding teachers whose ideas never diffuse throughout the school organization. These pockets of outstanding teachers are often called *islands of excellence.* In a truly effective K–12 learning school system, however, new educational innovations or best practices will diffuse from localized islands of excellence to other teachers throughout the school system.

In a K–12 learning school system

- Teachers share their best practices with colleagues in their work groups, and help each other gain proficiency
- Teachers are encouraged to find or develop new innovative solutions to educational problems
- School and district administrators support the diffusion of best practices and new innovations throughout the school system

In Chapter 7, we introduced the work of Everett Rogers, one of the world's foremost authorities on the diffusion of innovations. He defined *innovation* as

> the process through which an individual (or other decision-making unit) passes from first knowledge of an innovation to forming an attitude toward the innovation, to a decision to adopt or reject, to implementation and use of the new idea, and to confirmation of this decision. (2003, p. 475)

In 2003, Rogers reported there were more than 5,200 studies on the diffusion of ideas and products by individuals or organizations. Since the diffusion of ideas or products in an organization is a social change, and not specific to any particular field, we are confident that the stages of change identified by Yankelovich, Hall, Kotter, and Rogers, which we discussed in Chapter 7, are applicable to diffusion of ideas or practices in a school or school system. We have combined their work into three stages of diffusion that have the following characteristics:

- Stage 1: The awareness/innovation stage
- Stage 2: The learning/resistance/working-through stage
- Stage 3: The integration stage

In the pages that follow, we will describe each stage more fully as it relates to changes within one specific school. At the end of the chapter, we will discuss how superintendents can nurture the diffusion of innovative practices throughout an entire school system.

THE DIFFUSION OF INNOVATIVE PRACTICES WITHIN ONE SCHOOL

Stage 1: The Awareness/Innovation Stage

The awareness/innovation stage is the phase in which teachers first become aware of ideas that could help them improve their educational practice. In most cases, new ideas or best practices are learned from fellow colleagues or from external sources. In other cases, a teacher or group of teachers may create a new innovative solution to improve the school or classroom instruction.

Sometimes this stage is called the talking stage or piloting stage (see Figure 7.1 in Chapter 7). Since these new practices are completely voluntary, and no one else is expected to change his or her teaching practice, resistance from other faculty members is usually low or nonexistent.

Without a clear plan by school administrators to nurture continuous professional improvement for every teacher, the level of sharing ideas and creating new solutions is left to luck. In order to increase the level of innovation and ideas shared among colleagues, we urge administrators to *create conditions* that will support teacher innovation and encourage the sharing of best practices among teachers and to *support innovation champions*.

The Four Conditions

There are four conditions that are vital to creating an environment of innovation and shared best practices in schools. School leaders who foster adult learning in their schools

1. articulate their values and beliefs;

2. establish common planning time for teachers;

3. offer professional development opportunities both during and after the workday; and

4. use faculty meetings to share important educational ideas.

Condition 1: Administrators Are Clear About What They Believe and Value, and Act on Those Beliefs

If administrators truly value continuous professional development for all educators every day, then they must use every means possible to repeat their message frequently. One great speech on opening day is not sufficient. Similarly, just publishing the administrator's core values on the school's website will have no impact on anyone's beliefs or behavior. School leaders must take every opportunity to articulate their beliefs and values both in writing as well as when speaking with teachers, parents, and community members. School leaders also must behave in ways that demonstrate to others that they believe what they say. Teachers are more likely to follow school leaders who can articulate their vision, explain why the vision is best for the school, and inspire confidence that they have the will and capacity to actualize the vision.

Condition 2: Administrators Create Common Planning Time for Teachers During the Workday

It is not reasonable to expect most teachers to collaborate with colleagues after the workday. Most teachers have other obligations after school hours. If administrators truly believe in the value of teacher collaboration, then they must work with colleagues, and the union, to find ways to revise the master schedule so that teachers can meet in teams during the workday (such as grade level teams and subject area teams). According to Roland Barth, the former director of the Principals' Center at Harvard University,

> A precondition for doing *anything* to strengthen our practice and improve a school is the existence of a collegial culture in which professionals talk about practice, share their craft knowledge, and observe and root for the success of one another. Without these in place, no meaningful improvement—no staff or curriculum development, no teacher leadership, no student appraisal, no team teaching, no parent involvement, and no sustained change—is possible. (2006, p. 13)

Condition 3: Administrators Provide a Wide Array of Professional Development Opportunities for Teachers During and After the School Day

Creating professional learning communities (PLCs) during the workday is one of the best ways for teachers to share and learn from one another. In addition, we strongly recommend that administrators establish a committee of teachers and administrators whose members ask teachers what specific professional development they need to help them address current student needs. The goal of the school- or system-based professional development committee is to identify district-sponsored courses offered after regular school hours and school-sponsored professional development offered during the school day that will help teachers more effectively address student needs.

In order to ensure that the professional development opportunities actually change instruction and affect student learning, we strongly recommend that the professional development committee request anonymous surveys from teachers. The surveys should ask at least these three questions:

1. Did the professional development opportunity increase your teaching skills? If so, please describe how the program changed your teaching. If not, please describe why the program was not helpful.

2. Did student learning increase as a result of the application of knowledge gained from the professional development opportunity? If so, what evidence do you have?

3. How can the professional development program be improved for future participants?

Condition 4: Administrators Use Faculty Meetings to Share Important Educational Ideas

When principals set aside valuable time at faculty meetings to share ideas and invite faculty discussions, they model the very behavior they want their teachers to exhibit in their own teams (discussing and debating ideas, modeling high functioning team facilitation, raising questions, building shared knowledge, providing support to colleagues, and planning next steps). Faculty meetings allow the principal the opportunity to talk about his or her educational values and beliefs (Condition 1), to connect these values and beliefs to the practical life of the school, and to engage the entire faculty in serious discussions about how the whole team can improve teaching and learning in their school. Although in a learning school system there is never enough time for teachers to share their ideas, the faculty meeting is one effective tool the principal can use to honor teachers and encourage them to share their ideas with colleagues.

Some principals also use faculty meetings to discuss important educational issues, to bring in outside speakers, to engage the teachers in discussion of a book that everyone has read, or to set aside time for teachers to break into small work or discussion groups to discuss a topic or problem to be solved. In each case, the principal uses the time to increase the capacity of the entire school as a team and diffuse best practices throughout the school.

Innovation Champions

In order to increase the level of innovation and ideas shared among colleagues, we recommend that administrators support innovation champions in their schools. An innovation champion is "a charismatic individual who throws his or her weight behind an innovation, thus overcoming indifference or resistance that the new idea may provoke in an organization" (Rogers, 1995, p. 414). In 1963, researcher Donald Schön wrote in the *Harvard Business Review* that "Given the underground resistance to change . . . the new idea either finds a champion or dies" (p. 84). Schön argued that major changes within an organization must be backed by a champion who will advocate the idea as his or her own, promote the idea, and be willing to risk his or her position and prestige to advocate for the idea.

Schön's statement in 1963 is just as true today in schools as it was in business organizations 50 years ago. In a school or school system, all major changes need a strong advocate who can articulate why the changes are needed and who is willing to exert the energy and influence needed to bring about those changes. Schools are highly standardized organizations with numerous rules and traditions that are often difficult to overcome.

In a learning school system, most new ideas will be minor adjustments and won't require significant advocacy by a champion. However, there will be times when some faculty member or staff members will come forward with a proposal that would benefit children and would require a significant change in an academic program or in the school structure. As we discussed in Chapter 7, once a major change is seriously discussed as a real possibility, it is normal that some colleagues will question the change and, most likely, some will oppose it.

With our combined experience of over 60 years as school administrators, we are certain that leading change takes courage, energy, and passion. Major changes in school systems happen because someone is an innovation champion. That champion can be a teacher-leader, department head, principal, or superintendent of schools. According to Rogers, an innovation champion occupies a key linking position in his or her organization, has the analytical and intuitive skills to understand various individuals' aspirations, and demonstrates well-honed interpersonal and negotiating skills in working with other people in the organization (1995, p. 415).

As school leaders, we must either be the innovation champion ourselves when significant new ideas emerge or support the person (or persons) who will lead the change. Without our leadership and support, significant change is unlikely.

STAGE 2: THE LEARNING/RESISTANCE/ WORKING-THROUGH STAGE (OR PRE-DECISION STAGE THROUGH IMPLEMENTATION STAGE)

The learning/resistance/working-through stage is when most good ideas or innovations will either flourish or die. This is the phase when change advocates will encounter sincere suggestions, tough questions, harsh criticisms, and, from some faculty members, outright opposition. This is the phase when effective leaders must embrace the pushback from colleagues as part of the school's learning process rather than viewing it as one more obstacle to overcome.

The authors chose to name this stage the learning/resistance/working-through stage, since adults need time to first learn about a proposed change, state their objections, and then work through what the proposed change will mean for them. In a top-down administration that forces change, the administrator may get compliance but is unlikely to get support and deep understanding. However, in a learning school system, faculty members are given the time to discuss and debate why a proposed change is needed, how it will impact them, what they are expected to do differently, whether they support or object to the new initiative, and what support they will receive during the period of implementation. If sufficient time is allowed for the working-through stage, then faculty members are able to identify potential problems and make improvements.

In the learning/resistance/working-through stage (Stage 2), we recommend six strategies to help administrators bring new ideas from the beginning of the learning stage through successful implementation. The six strategies are:

1. Choose High-Leverage Starting Points

2. Communicate, Communicate, Communicate Very Clearly

3. Remove Obstacles During the Learning/Resistance/Working-Through Stage

4. Provide Teachers and Administrators With the Support They Need Before Launching an Initiative and During the Period of Implementation

5. Don't Be Afraid of the Implementation Dip

6. Celebrate Successes, Be Honest About Setbacks, and Build Confidence

In the pages that follow, we will discuss each of these strategies in detail, providing examples for each.

1. Choose High-Leverage Starting Points

Give me a place to stand and with a lever I will move the whole world

—Archimedes

Think back to when you were first appointed as a school principal, district administrator, or superintendent of schools. During that first year, you were energized to use your new role to improve education in your school or school system. As the new educational leader, you met with numerous people, asked about the organization's needs, and worked with colleagues to develop an action plan to improve the organization. Now, after considerable thought and dialogue with others, you announced your action plan and began the work with colleagues.

What is an action plan? In essence, it's a document that articulates the goal or goals to be accomplished, the implementation steps, timelines, and means of measurement. It is a set of goals based on the leader's understanding of how the school or school system works. At best, an action plan is a thoughtfully calculated gamble based both on years of experience in the field and on research.

As school administrators, we make decisions every day based on a set of assumptions that our decisions will produce intended outcomes. Or more simply put, we place bets. We make calculated bets that if we do X, then Y will happen. For example, if we hire a certain teacher, then his or her students will get an excellent education. If we give teachers common planning time to collaborate, and if these teachers review student work on a regular basis and modify their daily instruction, then more students will succeed in their classes.

According to Donella Meadows, who was an expert on systems thinking, there is no silver bullet, miracle cure, secret passage, magic password, or nearly effortless way to cut through or leap over huge obstacles. Meadows advocated that leaders look for high-leverage points, which she defined as "places within a complex system (a corporation, an economy, a living body, a city, an ecosystem) where a small shift in one thing can produce big changes in everything" (2009, p. 1).

As a school leader, our job is to choose the right high-leverage points that we believe are likely to produce intended results. In a learning school or school system, faculty members will likely promote more good ideas than time or resources will allow. Given the overload of good ideas to consider, we recommend that administrators evaluate faculty recommendations based on the following criteria:

- Choose initiatives that are likely to have a large impact on the school or school system
- Choose initiatives that are linked to school and district goals
- Choose only a small number of initiatives. Too many initiatives will lead to initiative fatigue and limited success
- Go for deep implementation
- Be prepared to spend years refining and implementing the initiatives. (Systems are highly complex and you may get it wrong.)

2. Communicate, Communicate, Communicate Very Clearly

Once a school leader decides which promising high-leverage initiative to present to the faculty, the next job is to communicate the initiative to others. At this stage of the learning/resistance/working-through process, the leader has an opportunity to help others learn why the change is needed, what the change is, and how the change will be implemented. Failure to communicate all three parts of the message will likely reduce a faculty's commitment to the proposed change and its ability to implement the change effectively. Below, we explain the importance of each part of the communication message more fully.

Communicating Why Change Is Needed

When a leader is able to clearly describe his or her vision and why a proposed change is needed, listeners are much more likely to embrace the proposed change. According to former Harvard Business School professor John Kotter, "a vision, a clever strategy or logical plan can rarely inspire the kind of action needed to produce change" (Kotter, 1996, p. 71). However, a vision combined with a compelling rationale (the *why*) can powerfully move people to embrace the proposed change.

Dr. Martin Luther King, Jr., was a master of combining vision with an explanation of why change is needed. For example, in his *I Have a Dream* speech, Dr. King brilliantly used words to communicate his vision. Nine times he declares his vision for America, each time starting with the phrase, "I have a dream . . . ," and concludes with

> And when this happens, when we allow freedom to ring, when we let it ring from every village and every hamlet, from every state and every city, we will be able to speed up that day when all of God's children, black men and white men, Jews and Gentiles, Protestants and Catholics, will be able to join hands and sing in the words of the old Negro spiritual, "Free at last! Free at last! Thank God Almighty, we are free at last!" (King, 1963)

And, Dr. King also answered the question "why" by stating that America has defaulted on its guarantee that all men are created equal and endowed by their creator with rights to "Life, Liberty, and the Pursuit of Happiness," as written in the Declaration of Independence.

However, if Dr. King had stood on the Washington Mall and given an "I have a plan" speech that articulated what we need to do and how to implement the plan, we seriously doubt many people would have responded passionately to the speech. Answering the question *why* is a powerful motivator (Sinek, 2009).

Communicating What Change Is Needed and How Change Will Be Implemented

Once a decision is made to implement a new initiative, it is obvious that the school leader must clearly communicate *what* will change and *how* the change will be implemented. Failure to effectively communicate the "what" and "how" to all affected employees will ensure the proposed change won't succeed. In addition, effectively communicating the "what" and "how" reduces faculty instability, uncertainty, and stress (Nadler, 1988, pp. 86–87). David Nadler, who was a consultant to CEOs of major corporations, found that instability, uncertainty, and stress will sap the very energy employees need to implement a needed change. However, he states that when change is handled well it can generate enormous excitement about "being part of a reinvigorated organization" (p. 87).

We also recommend that when school administrators communicate the "what" and the "how," they

- Keep the message clear, jargon-free, and focused
- Repeat, repeat, repeat their message to ensure the message is heard and understood. For example, when on September 8, 2011, President Obama addressed a joint session of Congress on the need to pass a jobs bill, he repeated the word *jobs* sixteen times

- Engage in two-way dialogue with all employees. Two-way communication is much more effective than one-way communication and it demonstrates respect for others
- Walk the walk. If the message does not match the leader's behavior, change is doomed
- Provide clear and manageable implementation steps. Great leaders know how to make ambitious goals look doable (Kotter, 1996, p. 75)

3. Remove Obstacles During the Learning/Resistance/Working-Through Stage

After the school leader has chosen a high-leverage strategy and explained it to his or her faculty, he or she is likely to run into significant obstacles. In Chapter 7, we discussed 41 specific obstacles to change. For a more detailed analysis, we urge the reader to take the self-directed audit test at the end of that chapter.

In this section, we discuss the three major categories of obstacles to change: (1) You're the person stopping change; (2) other people are stopping change; and (3) other, nonhuman obstacles are stopping change. We highlight the major themes within each category.

You're the Person Stopping Change

Congratulations—you have launched a learning organization. Worthwhile ideas are bubbling up around you, you have supported innovation champions, and now faculty members are expecting you to lead. Will you? There is no simple answer to this question. In Chapter 7, we identified six obstacles that could hold back even well-respected leaders when presented with recommendations that could improve their organization. The six obstacles are: personal capacity, personal risk, political risk, practicality, emotional impact, and social impact.

As school leaders in a learning organization, we have two responsibilities: first, to use our resources to provide the best possible education within the given organizational structure; and second, to continuously seek ways to improve the school. While the second responsibility is a core value, it is not a license to implement initiatives that you are not prepared to lead. If, after a careful examination of the six personal obstacles, you determine that implementing the recommended change is not possible or wise, then the prudent decision is to either slow down the change until the human or physical resources are available or reject the change. Our bias is toward action. Before rejecting worthwhile changes recommended by your faculty members, we urge readers to carefully consider each question listed at the end of Chapter 7. We suggest you carefully consider whether there is a way, perhaps with support from others, to overcome each personal obstacle.

Other People Are Stopping Change

Now that you have decided to proceed with a new initiative, what do you do when other people try to stop the change? In a learning organization with a culture of trust, the school leader should start by asking objectors why they oppose the proposed change. Their answers may suggest that you need to do a better job describing the vision and reteaching why change is needed. It is reasonable to expect that some faculty members will find fault with the implementation plan or believe the initiative won't work. If these are the objections, part of the learning process is to listen carefully to their concerns and "work through" the objections, if possible.

The two-way dialogue process we recommend is more than seeking what is often called "buy-in." Sincere two-way dialogue will demonstrate respect and should lead to deep understanding and more effective implementation.

However, sometimes other people have values or interests that will cause them to object to the proposed change. For example, suppose you decide that you need to reallocate the school budget to serve the needs of a group of struggling students, and that will mean cuts in programs that will affect certain faculty members or parents. In this case, the parents or union members whose programs will receive less financial support may oppose the change even if they agree with its goals. Here is where your leadership may be tested. If, after dialogue, you decide that the change you're advocating is still needed, then you will need to use your prestige, courage, and political skills to push your agenda.

Other Obstacles Are Stopping Change

Sometimes there are very practical, nonhuman obstacles that will stop change. For example, school leaders attempting to institute change will often encounter legal obstacles, contractual constraints, lack of finances, insufficient staff, or other structural impediments. Before proceeding with an initiative, wise administrators will study the implementation plan to make sure they have the resources they need, or can reasonably obtain them, as they advocate for the desired change. In Section 4, we will discuss how to approach faculty resistance.

4. Provide Teachers and Administrators With the Support They Need Before Launching an Initiative and During the Period of Implementation

In order to help bring teachers and administrators from the beginning of the learning stage through successful implementation of a new initiative, it is important for supervisors to provide employees with the support they need both before launching a new initiative and during its implementation. Lack of support from supervisors is one of the major reasons that faculty members and administrators will resist or reject a new idea. Sixty years of research on the diffusion of innovation shows that most people are cautious and need time to evaluate a proposed change that will impact their personal or professional lives (Rogers, 2005). As discussed in Chapter 7, Rogers and others found that for any particular innovation, approximately 84% of the population are not innovators or early adopters.

Asking staff members to significantly change their professional practice without providing them responsible support will likely result in resistance. In the *Superintendent's Fieldbook*, James Harvey and Gene Hall explain why it is impractical to expect staff members who lack support to make the "leap of faith"—to jump over a chasm they call "today's ugly reality" on one side of a cliff to "tomorrow's beautiful possibility" on the other side (Hall & Harvey, 2004). Harvey states that "They may like you. They may even think you are a wonderful person. And if you want to make the leap over the chasm and crash and burn, you will make the leap with their best wishes. But only a few will be inclined to jump off the cliff with you" (p. 220). Please see Figure 8.1.

Figure 8.1

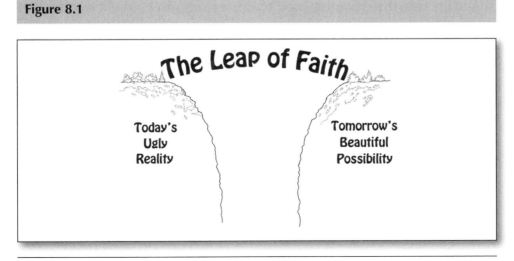

Source: Hall, Gene E., & Hord, Shirley M., *Implementing Change: Patterns, Principles, and Potholes*, 1st edition, © 2001. Reprinted by permission of Pearson Education, Inc., Upper Saddle River, NJ.

We cannot emphasize enough that many administrators seriously underestimate the amount of time and professional development that educators need to make a significant change in practice. A 2009 study found that educators require an average of about 50 hours or more of intensive and sustained professional development on a given topic to produce changes in practices that result in gains in student achievement (Wei et al., 2009).

In addition, some faculty members need time to let go of familiar surroundings and practices. In a study of transformational leadership, Tichy and Devanna found that

> in managing the rational and socioemotional conflicts associated with resistance to change in industrial firms, the senior managers must summarize the past and eulogize its value, as well as emphasize the continuities of the past with the future and justify the changes. (Bass, 1990, p. 289)

5. Don't Be Afraid of the Implementation Dip

Administrators should expect that once a new initiative is launched, faculty members will most likely need to learn new skills, knowledge, and ways of interacting with others. While some faculty members will adapt to the new paradigm quickly, others may experience fear of personal failure, fear that their students will suffer, or anger at the supervisor who forced them to change. These educators may feel like they made the leap of faith, jumped across the chasm, missed the other side, and will smash into the abyss deep below.

Once the implementation process has begun, during the next six to twelve months school leaders should expect reduced performance and considerable faculty unrest. This period, which is commonly called the *implementation dip*, is when faculty members make the transition from old practices they know well to new practices they have not yet mastered. It is during this time period that the impact of the change process may cause faculty fear and anxiety, given their lack of technical skills and knowledge during the first year of transition. Our experience has shown that the overall level of employee performance typically declines for approximately six months before rising to even greater performance after eighteen months, once new skills and routines are learned. (Please see Figure 8.2.)

Figure 8.2 The Implementation Dip

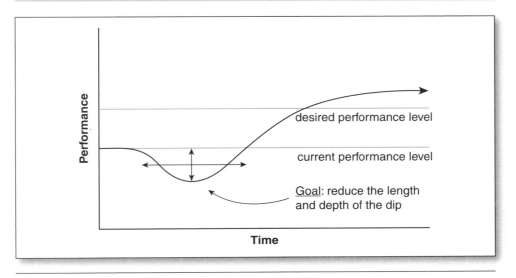

Source: McLeod, Scott, 2007, "Implementation Dip." Retrieved from http://dangerouslyirrelevant
.org/2007/07/implementation.html

It is not uncommon for school leaders to experience a backlash from faculty members who never liked the change in the first place, and from other faculty members who blame administrators for their frustrations. We can often forget that learning is difficult even for highly competent teachers, who may resent or blame others for their feelings of insecurity during the implementation dip. During the implementation dip, we urge school administrators to provide substantial support to their faculty members and to frequently acknowledge and praise them as they demonstrate new skills. Most school administrators seriously underestimate the level of support all adults need as they learn new complex ways of working with colleagues or of teaching.

For example, in 2005 in Lexington, Massachusetts, one of the coauthors of this book, the new superintendent of schools, conducted extensive interviews to learn about the school system. He quickly learned that the vast majority of teachers worked in isolation and made autonomous decisions about what was taught. Given that the new superintendent believed the district needed to create a collaborative culture to improve the overall quality of teaching, he made the decision to launch PLCs. The transition included the creation of mandatory common planning time each week for teachers who taught the same grade or subject and the expectation that these teachers would collaborate to improve their teaching and student learning. Six months into the change, there was a backlash from the union. Teachers posted on the union's website how much they disliked being required to meet with colleagues during the day. Some teachers were uncomfortable discussing their students' progress with others. Other teachers did not know what to do during the common planning period.

Amazingly, about six months later, faculty opinion radically changed and became much more positive. About 18 months after the change, almost all faculty members said they supported PLCs and would object if the administration ever abolished PLCs and they had to go back to isolation in their classrooms.

Even though the administration and faculty members were pleased 18 months after making the leap to a PLC model, the transition would have been far easier if the district had provided much more professional development to principals and teachers and had acknowledged and praised teachers as they learned new collaboration skills.

Once a major change has been implemented, administrators should expect some pushback from faculty members even with adequate support and praise. In order to keep the initiative moving forward through the learning/resistance/working-through stage, administrators will need to keep the vision in front of all teachers, frequently explain why the new model is better than the old model, and demonstrate intestinal fortitude when staff members blame them for their frustrations. During this difficult time, administrators should maintain two-way communication with faculty, adjust practices and timetables if needed, and should not fear the implementation dip.

6. Celebrate Successes, Be Honest About Setbacks, and Build Confidence

What does it feel like when you work hard, learn something new, and get significant results? You're proud of yourself and feel great. It doesn't matter whether the new skill is hitting a ball over a tennis net, learning how to use a #3 wood in golf, or learning to use a new technology in the classroom. Working hard and learning a new skill feels good.

Harvard Business School Professor Rosabeth Moss Kanter, in her book titled *Confidence*, found that when employees get results, it builds employee confidence that more success is possible, which then leads to even more success (Kanter, 2004). Celebrating success after success energizes people to work harder, push through the implementation dip, and learn to implement the new initiative at higher and higher levels.

Since individual and organizational confidence is based on actual achievement, school leaders must remember that celebrating small wins builds confidence. They also must be honest about setbacks, provide staff significant support during this learning phase, and keep repeating why the goal is important. According to Kanter, it is no accident that companies and sports teams with long winning streaks celebrate their successes and acknowledge their setbacks without blame: "Winning feels good and good moods are contagious" (p. 29).

While acknowledging success at all times is important, providing support during a period of change is essential. Saying "Thank you" does not require a budget or take much time out of your busy day. For example, handwritten thank-you notes are extremely powerful motivators. Some teachers keep them in their desks for years. At the end of the day, we recommend you take a few minutes to send a teacher or two a note acknowledging some accomplishment. You both will feel better and your note will build confidence.

STAGE 3: THE INTEGRATION STAGE

The integration stage occurs when there is intellectual and emotional acceptance, transformation, and anchoring of the change by the stakeholders. In the third stage, stakeholders accept the change, its rationale, and the pros and cons. The new initiative becomes an ongoing part of the school's activities and identity.

In our discussion of the third stage, we examine two strategies to cement a successful initiative into the daily life of the school: (1) monitoring progress with continued support, and (2) allowing enough time for the transition to become permanently embedded in the school's culture. While it is possible that the new initiative may survive on its own at the end of Stage 2, the change may be too fragile to withstand future challenges and a change in leadership. Stage 3 is designed to increase educator confidence and competence and to ensure lasting change.

Monitor Progress and Provide Continued Support to Faculty Members

What do music teachers, athletic coaches, and video games have in common? All three provide specific and immediate feedback to students, which helps them improve performance. In the music classroom and on the athletic field, the teacher or coach's job is to monitor each student's behavior and then tell the student what he or she needs to change to improve performance. In a role-playing video game, the player must fight some monster or solve some puzzle in order to avoid some event that will kill their character. However, the good news is that the player of the video game can try again: He or she can learn from his or her mistake and, after "dying," can restart the game and play the scene over and over again until he or she masters the challenge.

Providing immediate and specific feedback is a powerful way to increase the depth and pace of student learning. In a study of 300 schools, Douglas Reeves reported that "schools with the highest monitoring scores have more than five times the gains in student achievement than schools with the lowest monitoring scores" (Reeves, 2009, p. 109). Reeves identified four characteristics of effective monitoring practices: frequency, specificity, measurability, and comprehensiveness. Robert Waterman and Tom Peters, in their bestselling business book, *In Search of Excellence*, came to the same conclusion when they penned the phrase "What gets measured gets done" (1982).

We contend that the importance of monitoring, as described by Reeves, Waterman, and Peters, also applies to school leaders who sincerely wish to improve their faculty members' skills. Teachers are no different than the student in the music class, the athlete on the ball field, or the player of a video game. All educators need specific and frequent feedback when learning new skills.

In addition to providing specific and frequent monitoring, all learners, including adults, need considerable support during the change process. As described earlier in this chapter, Hall and Harvey made the following comparison: asking teachers to support and implement a large change without support (professional development) is like asking them to jump over the chasm, to make a "Leap of Faith" and hope they won't fall into the abyss.

In another article, Hall recommends that school leaders build an "implementation bridge" from one side of the "chasm" to the other (Hall & Hord, 2011). These authors use a bridge as a metaphor for the professional development teachers need to grow from "not knowing the new skill" (low level of implementation) to "competent practice" (high levels of implementation).

Providing professional development needs to start at a low level in Stage 2, when the new initiative is first discussed. That's when teachers will ask, "What is the new change?," "Why is it needed?," and "How will it affect me?"

As the change is implemented, all teachers will need ongoing support and feedback to help them make the change effectively. Finally, in Stage 3, as teachers move out of the implementation dip toward high levels of implementation, support should become more targeted for those teachers who need it. Finally, when almost all faculty members have crossed the implementation bridge, school leaders can redirect the professional supports to new teachers and to those few remaining teachers who still require help.

Change is complicated and sometimes frightening. To help all adult learners make the journey across the implementation bridge, effective school leaders must monitor the change process, determine successes and failures, identify what supports teachers need, and celebrate successes along the way to build pride and confidence. In a K–12 learning organization, our goal is learning for all adults so that they can more effectively educate all children.

Do Not Expect Quick Results—Creating Effective and Deep Change Is a Marathon, Not a Sprint

As school leaders, we live in a world of contradictions. We are sometimes expected to solve tough educational problems very quickly without the public's recognition that American schools were designed to remain stable and standardized. As leaders, we are passionate about improving our schools or school systems, yet we know that school organizations are complex social systems that change very slowly. We know that school leaders who change schools too quickly may be pushed over for failing to maintain the expectation of stability. We also know that school leaders who challenge people too slowly may be seen as weak, ineffective leaders.

How does a school leader reconcile the two opposing forces: the urgent need for change and the reality that effective and deep change can take years to accomplish?

As we previously discussed, we suggested that school leaders reject the tyranny of *or* and embrace the genius of *and*. We recommend that school leaders combine the urgency of launching change immediately with careful planning, implementation, monitoring, and professional development. At the same time, school leaders must accept that deep and effective change will take a long time to accomplish. While this may seem like a contradiction, it is not. Few people demand that the entire scope of a real problem be solved immediately. Rather, teachers, parents, and board members admire leaders who understand their needs and can implement a plan that gets results over a reasonable time period.

Instead of thinking that complex problems can be solved quickly, it is more important that the leader inspire others to embrace the vision and believe that the journey will improve the lives of students. Followers need to know that they will have the leader's support throughout the difficult change process, and that their leaders are committed to what they say as evidenced by their consistent deeds over many years. Followers need time to innovate, time to decide which innovations will address their needs, time to work through resistance and problems, and time to embed the new practices into the routines of the school. According to Rogers, time is involved in diffusion of innovations.

As school leaders, we are in powerful positions to improve the lives of students by changing the way all educators work every day. In a K–12 learning school system, we set the conditions to help all educators learn to improve practice every day, every year, and long after we retire. The goal is continuous improvement, not quick results. Effective change is not a sprint; it is a marathon.

DIFFUSING INNOVATIONS FROM ONE SCHOOL TO THE ENTIRE SCHOOL SYSTEM— WHOLE SCHOOL SYSTEM CHANGE

The model presented in this chapter describes how an individual principal or school leader can lead change in his or her school—from the awareness/innovation stage through the learning/resistance/working-through stage and into the integration stage. The final section of this book examines the transition from individual school change to whole school system change.

Great ideas and innovations can diffuse throughout a school system at any time. The diffusion process is not dependent on whether a new, promising practice has just started within one school or has already been in place for years. Great ideas and practices will diffuse throughout a school system if there are multiple communication channels for the spread of ideas, practices, and innovations (Rogers, 1995, p. 18). Rogers defines a "communication channel" as "the means by which messages get from one individual to another" (p. 17). The more communication channels that exist within a school system, the more likely great ideas will spread to all schools and take root. For example, four common channels are

- a districtwide administrator who learns about an innovation or practice from a principal and shares the information with other principals;
- a principal who regularly meets with other principals who share their promising practices with one another;
- an individual teacher serving on a systemwide collaborative team who shares a promising practice with a teacher in another school;
- an educator who shares a promising practice with a colleague who is engaged in the same or similar work.

One example of how an innovation can spread throughout a school and school system very rapidly is through the introduction of a new and effective technology. For example, in one Boston school system, the local parent education foundation bought two ELMO document cameras for each of the six elementary schools. (An ELMO document camera is a device by which a teacher may show objects or documents to the entire class by placing them under the camera, which projects the image onto a screen.) Within months of the purchase of the ELMO cameras, each of the twelve teachers who received one were raving about the multiple ways they could use the new technology in their classrooms and about how this new technology improved their teaching. One teacher told colleagues that the device could be connected to a microscope and now she could show microscopic organisms on a screen to the entire class. Another teacher shared with colleagues that he was now able to put a book or worksheet under the document reader and show the printed material to all students at the same time.

The demand for the innovative technology spread very quickly. Fellow teachers were very impressed. Parents began demanding that the PTAs use their funds to buy more ELMOs. The PTAs began writing letters to the school board requesting that the district buy more ELMOs. Within one year, the school system had used end-of-the-year surplus funds to buy every Grade 1 through Grade 5 teacher in all six of its elementary schools an ELMO projector.

In a K–12 learning school system, new practices or innovations can diffuse two ways: school-to-school or from the central office to all schools. In the school-to-school case, each time the new idea travels to a new school, the three stages of diffusion described above begin again. Once teachers become aware of the new practice or innovation in another school, the principal must still communicate why the change is needed, what the change will mean, and how the school will provide professional support and monitor success. The second, third, and fourth schools that then adopt the change must also go through the learning/resistance/working-through stage until there is deep integration. The change process is a learning process for every school, no matter how successful it was in another school.

The other way that new practices or innovations can diffuse is from the central office to all schools. In this case, a district administrator serves as the innovation champion who marshals resources, communicates why the change is needed, and coordinates the K–12 efforts to make the change happen. A central office administrator may become the innovation champion if the school system must make changes in a districtwide collective bargaining agreement, if school board support is needed to make the change, or if the administrator decides that school-to-school change would be too slow to address major needs of the school system.

FINAL THOUGHTS

The book began with a question: How do we increase educator capacity in order to provide a more effective education for all students in all schools? While there are many factors that contribute to effective schools, we conclude that creating a K–12 learning organization for the adults is the most effective way to improve student learning. If the adults don't change their behaviors from current practices, then no increase in the school budget or change in school structures will matter. Ultimately, what matters is the quality of teaching in the classroom every day.

As school leaders for over 60 combined years, we have concluded that hiring smart, well-trained, and hardworking teachers is important; however, it won't enable school districts to provide the best possible education given their resources so long as teachers act in isolation. Even the best teachers have limits as to what they can accomplish individually in a classroom. However, if we break down the walls of teacher isolation, build a culture of trust, collaboration, and leadership, and provide high-quality capacity-building activities, then all teachers will improve their practice. These four drivers of change will act synergistically and enable educators to generate new educational solutions for their students. Finally, if school leaders are willing to become the innovation champions in their schools or school systems, then great ideas and practices will diffuse throughout a school system, which will lead to more teachers generating more ideas every day to improve teaching and learning and more effective K–12 classroom instruction for *all* students.

References

Argyris, C., Putnam, R., & Smith, D. M. (1985). *Action science*. San Francisco: Jossey-Bass.

Balkin, J., & Rodriguez, C. (n.d.). *An interactive civil rights chronology.* Retrieved from http://www.yale.edu/lawweb/jbalkin/brown/1964.html

Barth, R. S. (2002). The culture builder. *Educational Leadership*, *59*(8), 6–11.

Barth, R. S. (2006). Improving relationships within the schoolhouse. *Educational Leadership*, *63*(6), 8–13.

Bass, B. M. (1990). *Bass and Stogdill's handbook of leadership* (3rd ed.). New York: Free Press.

Berry, B., Daughtrey, A., & Wieder, A. (2010). *Developing a better system for schools: Developing, supporting and retaining teachers*. Hillsborough, NC: Center for Teaching Quality.

Bryk, A. S., & Schneider, B. (2002). *Trust in schools: A core resource for improvement*. New York: Russell Sage Foundation.

Bryk, A. S., & Schneider, B. (2003). Trust in schools: A core resource for school reform. *Educational Leadership*, *60*(6), 40–45.

Burkhart, V. (2007, November 12). *An interview with Keith Sawyer, author of* Group Genius. Idea Connection. Retrieved from http://www.ideaconnection.com/open-innovation-articles/00003-Group-Genius-Everyone-Can-be-More-Creative-But.html

Busick, K. U., & Inos, R. H. (1992). *Synthesis of the research on education change, part 2*. Honolulu, HI: Pacific Resources for Education and Learning.

California segregation laws. (2004). *Brown v. Board of Education: The Southern California perspective*. San Diego, CA: University of San Diego. Retrieved from http://sshl.ucsd.edu/brown/calcode.htm

Cambron-McCabe, N. H., Cunningham, L. L., Harvey, J., & Koff, R. H. (2004). *The superintendent's fieldbook: A guide for leaders of learning*. Thousand Oaks, CA: Corwin.

Chenoweth, K. (2007). *It's being done*. Cambridge, MA: Harvard Education Press.

Christensen, C., Horn, M., & Johnson, C. (2008). *Disrupting class: How disruptive innovation will change the way the world learns*. New York: McGraw-Hill.

Clifford, G. J. (1978). Words for schools: The applications in education of the vocabulary researches of Edward L. Thorndike. In P. Suppes (Ed.), *Impact of research on education: Some case studies* (pp. 107–198). Washington, DC: National Academy of Education.

Cohen, D. K., & Hill, H. (2001). *Learning policy: When state education reform works*. New Haven, CT: Yale University Press.

Collins, J., & Porras, J. (2002). *Built to last.* New York: HarperCollins.

Conant, J. B. (1959). *The American high school today.* New York: McGraw-Hill.

Corcoran, T. B. (1995). *Helping teachers teach well: Transforming professional development.* (CPRE Policy Brief). Philadelphia: Consortium for Policy Research in Education, Graduate School of Education, University of Pennsylvania. Retrieved from http://www2.ed.gov/pubs/CPRE/t61/t61c.html

Cremin, L. A. (1957). *The republic and the school: Horace Mann on the education of free men.* New York: Teachers College Press.

Darling-Hammond, L. (2000). Teacher quality and student achievement: A review of state policy evidence. *Education Policy Analysis Archives, 8*(1). Retrieved from http://epaa.asu.edu/ojs/article/view/392.

D'Auria, J. (2009). The superintendent as teacher. *Phi Delta Kappan, 91*(1), 81–83.

D'Auria, J. (2010) *Ten lessons in leadership and learning.* Wellesley, MA: Teachers21.

D'Auria, J., & King, M. (2009). A principal's dilemma. *Schools: Studies in Education, 6,* 129–137.

Davis, R. L. F. (n.d.) *Surviving Jim Crow: In-depth essay.* Retrieved from http://www.spodawg32.net/files/Surviving_Jim_Crow_PDF.pdf

Deninger, M. (2008, September). *Disproportionality: A look at special education and race in the Commonwealth (Educational Research Brief).* Malden, MA: Massachusetts Department of Elementary and Secondary Education. Retrieved from http://www.doe.mass.edu/research/reports/Edbrief_final.pdf

Dorn, S. (2012, July 4). *A nation of patriots, a nation of fandoms.* Boulder, CO: National Education Policy Center, University of Colorado. Retrieved from http://nepc.colorado.edu/blog/nation-patriots-nation-fandoms

Dufour, R., & Eaker, R. (1998): *Learning communities at work: Best practices for enhancing student achievement.* Bloomington, IN: Association for Supervision and Curriculum Development.

Dweck, C. (2006). *Mindset: The new psychology of success.* New York: Random House.

Dweck, C. (n.d.). *What is mindset?* Retrieved October 16, 2011 from http://mindsetonline.com/whatisit/about/index.html

Edmondson, A. (2007). *A fuller explanation: The synergetic geometry of R. Buckminster Fuller.* Pueblo, CO: Emergent World Press.

Eisner, E. (1983). The art and craft of teaching. *Educational Leadership, 40*(4), pp. 4–13.

Fractals. (n.d.) In Wikipedia. Retrieved January 30, 2011, from http://en.wikipedia.org/wiki/Fractals

Freeman, D. A. (2011, September 20.) *Online gamers solve HIV puzzle that stymied scientists.* CBS Interactive. Retrieved from http://www.cbsnews.com/8301-504763_162-20108763-10391704.html

Fuhrman, S. H., & Odden, A. (2001). Introduction: School reform. *Phi Delta Kappan, 83*(1), 59–61.

Fullan, M. (1993). *Change forces: Probing the depths of educational change.* London: Falmer Press.

Fullan, M. (2005). *Leadership and sustainability.* Thousand Oaks, CA: Corwin.

Fullan, M. (2008a). The six secrets of change. (Keynote presentation handout). Retrieved from http://www.michaelfullan.ca/resource_assets/handouts/08_Nov_Keynote_US.pdf

Fullan, M. (2008b). *The six secrets of change: What the best leaders do to help their organizations survive and thrive.* San Francisco: Jossey-Bass.

Fullan, M. (2010). *All systems go.* Thousand Oaks, CA: Corwin.

Fullan, M. (2011, April 2011). *Choosing the wrong drivers for whole school change.* (Seminar Series Paper No. 204). East Melbourne, Victoria, Australia: Center for Strategic Education.

Garet, M. S., Porter, A. C., Desimone, L., Birman, B., & Yoon, K. (2001). What makes professional development effective? Results from a national sample of teachers. *American Educational Research Journal, 38*(4), 915–945.

Gawande, A. (2007). *Better: A surgeon's notes on performance.* New York: Henry Holt.

Getzels, J. W. (1978). Paradigm and practice: On the impact of basic research in education. In P. Suppes (Ed.), *Impact of research on education: Some case studies* (pp. 477–521). Washington, DC: National Academy of Education.

Ginott, H. (1976). *Teacher and child: A book for parents and teachers.* New York: MacMillan.

Goodlad, J. (1983). *A place called school.* New York: McGraw-Hill.

Greenwald, R., Hedges, L.V., & Laine, R. D. (1996). The effects of school resources on student achievement. *Review of Educational Research, 66,* 361–396.

Hall, G. E., & Harvey, J. (2004). Stages of concern. In N. H. Cambron-McCabe, L. L. Cunningham, J. Harvey, & R. H. Koff, *The superintendent's fieldbook: A guide for leaders of learning* (pp. 220–223). Thousand Oaks, CA: Corwin.

Hall, G. E., & Hord, S. M. (2001). *Implementing change: Patterns, principles, and potholes.* Boston: Allyn & Bacon.

Hall, G. E., & Hord, S. M. (2011). Implementation: Learning builds the bridges between research and practice. *Journal of Staff Development, 32*(4), 52–57.

Hargreaves, A., & Fullan, M. (1992). *Understanding teacher development.* New York: Teachers College Press.

Hattie, J. (2009). *Visible learning: A synthesis of over 800 meta-analyses relating to achievement.* New York: Routledge.

Hattie, J. (2012). *Visible learning for teachers: Maximizing impact on learning.* New York: Routledge.

Hattie, J., & Timperley, H. (2007). Power of feedback. *Review of Educational Research, 77*(1), p. 81–112.

Heifetz, R. A. (1994). *Leadership without easy answers.* Cambridge, MA: Harvard University Press.

Hemphill, F. C., Vanneman, A., & Rahman, T. (2011). *Achievement gaps: How Hispanic and White students in public schools perform in mathematics and reading on the National Assessment of Educational Progress.* Washington, DC: National Center for Educational Statistics, Institute of Education Sciences, U.S. Department of Education. Retrieved from http://nces.ed.gov/nationsreportcard/pubs/studies/2011459.asp

Herzberg, F. (1987, September). One more time: How do you motivate employees? *Harvard Business Review.* (Originally published 1968). Retrieved from http://www.facilitif.eu/user_files/file/herzburg_article.pdf

Hoff, D. (2007). Views of AFT, NEA on reauthorization getting closer. *Education Week, 26*(28), 23.

Isaacson, W. (2011). *Steve Jobs.* New York: Simon and Shuster.

Joyce, B., & Showers, B. (1996). The evolution of peer coaching. *Educational Leadership, 53*(6), 12–16.

Joyce, B., & Showers, B. (2002). Student achievement through professional development. In B. Joyce & B. Showers (Eds.), *Designing training and peer coaching: Our need for learning.* Alexandria, VA: Association for Supervision and Curriculum Development.

Kanter, R. M. (2004). *Confidence: How winning streaks and losing streaks begin and end.* New York: Crown Business.

King, M. L. (1963). *"I Have a Dream" speech.* Retrieved from Public Broadcasting System, http://www.pbs.org/wnet/historyofus/web14/segment7b.html

Klein, A. (2011, April 1). Advocates worry ESEA rewrite may weaken law. *Education Week.* Retrieved from http://www.edweek.org/ew/articles/2011/04/01/27esea.h30.html

Kotter, J. (1996). *Leading change.* Cambridge, MA: Harvard Business School Press.

Kouzes, J. M., & Posner, B. Z. (2003). *Exemplary leadership.* San Francisco: Jossey-Bass.

LaMura, V. (2007, November). *The achievement gap in the Lexington Public Schools: Research and recommendations.* (Report submitted to the Lexington, Massachusetts School Committee.) Retrieved from http://lps.lexingtonma.org/cms/lib2/MA01001631/Centricity/Domain/565/AchievementGapRptJan08.pdf

Lau v. Nichols, 414 U.S. 563 (1974). Retrieved from http://caselaw.lp.findlaw.com/scripts/getcase.pl?court=us&vol=414&invol=563

Learning Forward. (2012). *Strategic plan.* Retrieved from http://www.learningforward.org/who-we-are/purpose-beliefs-priorities

Legal status of the colored population in respect to schools and education in each of the different States, with statistics of schools in each state. (1871). In *Special Report of the Commissioner of Education on the Condition and Improvement of Public Schools in the District of Columbia, Submitted to the Senate June, 1868, and to the House, with Additions June 13, 1870* (pp. 301–400). Washington, DC: U.S. Government Printing Office.

Lencioni, P. (2002). *The five dysfunctions of a team.* San Francisco: Jossey-Bass.

Levin, R. A. (1991). The debate over schooling: Influences of Dewey and Thorndike. *Childhood Education, 68*(2), 71–75.

Little, J. W. (1982). Norms of collegiality and experimentation: Workplace conditions of school success. *American Educational Research Journal, 19*(3), 325–340.

Lortie, D. (2002). *Schoolteacher.* Chicago: The University of Chicago.

Losen, D. J., & Orfield, G. (2002). *Racial inequity in special education.* Cambridge, MA: Harvard Educational Publishing Group.

Machiavelli, N. (1961). *The prince.* (G. Bull, Trans.). Baltimore: Penguin. (Original work published 1513)

Mandelbrot, B. B. (1982). *The fractal geometry of nature.* New York: W. H. Freeman.

Massachusetts Foundation for the Humanities. (2005, May 17). May 17, 1954: Supreme Court strikes down "separate but equal." *Mass Moments.* Retrieved from http://www.massmoments.org/moment.cfm?mid=146

McLeod, S. (2007, July 23). Implementation dip. *Dangerously Irrelevant: Technology, Leadership, and the Future of Schools* [blog]. Retrieved from http://dangerously irrelevant.org/2007/07/implementation.html

Meadows, D. (2009). Leverage points: Places to intervene in a system. *The Solutions Journal 1*(1). Retrieved from http://www.thesolutionsjournal.com/node/419

Meiers, M., & Ingvarson, L. (2005). *Investigating the links between teacher professional development and student learning outcomes* (Vol. 1). Camberwell, Victoria, Australia: Australian Council for Educational Research.

Mendro, R. L. (1998). Student achievement and school and teacher accountability. *Journal of Personnel Evaluation in Education, 12*(3), 257–267.

MetLife (2009). *MetLife survey of the American teacher: Collaborating for student success.* New York: Author.

Mitchell, C., & Sackney, L. (2000). *Profound improvement: Building capacity for a learning community.* Lisse, Netherlands: Swets & Zeitlinger.

Mitchell, C., & Sackney, L. (2001). Building capacity for a learning community. *Canadian Journal of Educational Administration and Policy, 19*(4).

Mourshed, M., Chijioke, C., & Barber, M. (2010). *How the most improved school systems keep getting better.* New York: McKinsey & Company.

Nadler, D. A. (1988). *Champions of change.* San Francisco: Jossey-Bass.

National Association of Secondary School Principals. (2004, June 29). *Shortage of qualified candidates hindering the improvement of schools.* [Press release]. Retrieved from http://www.nassp.org/Content.aspx?topic=25541

National Board for Professional Teaching Standards. (2012). *National Board Certification for Educational Leaders (NBCEL).* Arlington, VA: Author. Retrieved from http://www.nbpts.org/products_and_services/national_board_certifica1

National Center for Education Statistics. *Teacher professional development in 1999–2000: What teachers, principals, and district staff report.* (2006, January). Retrieved from http://nces.ed.gov/search/?output=xml_no_dtd&client=nces&site=nces&q=professional+development+2000

Oakes, J. (1986). Tracking, inequality and the rhetoric of reform: Why schools don't change. *Journal of Education, 168*(1), 60–80.

Parsad, B., Lewis, L., & Farris, E. (2001). *Teacher preparation and professional development: 2000* (NCES Publication No. 2001–088). Washington, DC: National Center for Educational Statistics.

Pennsylvania Association of Elementary and Secondary School Principals (2006, October 25). *Principal shortage looming in northeastern states.* [Press release]. Summerdale, PA: Author. Retrieved from http://www.paessp.org/publications/press-releases/2006/122-principal-shortage-looming-in-northeastern-states.html

Perkins, D. (2003) *King Arthur's Round Table: How collaborative conversations create smart organizations.* Hoboken, NJ: John Wiley.

Porter, A., Garet, M., Desimone, L., Yoon, K., & Birman, B., (2000). *Does professional development change teaching practice? Result from a three-year study.* Washington, DC: U.S. Department of Education.

Primary sources: America's teachers on America's schools. *A Project of the Bill & Melinda Gates Foundation.* (2010) Published at http://www.scholastic.com/primarysources/download.asp.

Professional development. (2011, June 29). *Education Week.* Retrieved from http://www.edweek.org/ew/issues/professional-development/

Rampbell, C. (2010, June 2). Graduation rates, by state and race. *New York Times.* Retrieved from http://economix.blogs.nytimes.com/2010/06/02/graduation-rates-by-state-and-race

Rating the management gurus. (2001, October 14). *Business Week.* Retrieved at http://www.businessweek.com/stories/2001-10-14/rating-the-management-gurus

Reeves, D. B. (2006, September). Pull the weeds before you plant the flowers. *Educational Leadership, 64*(1), pp. 89–90.

Reeves, D. B. (2009). *Assessing educational leaders* (2nd ed.). Thousand Oaks, CA: Corwin.

Reeves, D. B. (2010). *Transforming development into student results.* Alexandria, VA: ASCD.

Reiguluth, C., & Garfinkle, R. (1994). *Systemic change in education.* Englewood Cliffs, NJ: Educational Technology Publications.

Reina, M. L., & Reina, D. S. (2007). Building sustainable trust. *OD Practitioner, 39*(1), 36–41.

Robinson, K. (2006, February). *Ken Robinson says schools kill creativity.* [Video file]. Retrieved from http://www.ted.com/talks/ken_robinson_says_schools_kill_creativity.html

Rogers, E. (1995). *Diffusion of innovations* (4th ed.). New York: Free Press.

Rogers, E. (2003). *Diffusion of innovations.* (5th ed.). New York: Free Press.

Rosenholz, S. (1985). Effective schools: Interpreting the evidence. *American Journal of Education*, Vol. 93, No. 3, pp. 352–388.

Rothberg, R. (1986). Dealing with the problem of teacher isolation. *The Clearing House, 59*(7), 320–322.

Roza, M. (2003). *A matter of definition: Is there truly a shortage of school principals?* Seattle, WA: Center on Reinventing Public Education, Daniel J. Evans School of Public Affairs, University of Washington. Retrieved from http://www.wallacefoundation.org/knowledge-center/school-leadership/state-policy/Documents/Is-There-Truly-a-Shortage-of-School-Principals.pdf

Saphier, J., & D'Auria, J. (1993). *How to bring vision to school improvement.* Carlisle, MA: Research for Better Teaching.

Saphier, J., Haley-Speca, M. A., & Gower, R. (2008). *The skillful teacher.* Acton, MA: Research for Better Teaching.

Sawyer, K. (2007). *Group genius.* New York: Basic Books.

Schön, D. (1963). Champions for radical new information. *Harvard Business Review, 41,* 77–86.

Scientific management (definition). (2012). In Dictionary.com's 21st Century Lexicon. Retrieved from http://dictionary.reference.com/browse/scientific management

Seller, M. (1981). G. Stanley Hall and Edward Thorndike on the education of women: Theory and policy in the Progressive Era. *Educational Studies, 11*(4), 365–374.

Senge, P. (1996). *The leader of the future.* San Francisco: Jossey-Bass.

Senge, P. (2007). *The fifth discipline: The art and science of a learning organization.* New York: Doubleday.

Sergiovanni, T. (2000). *The lifeworld of leadership: Creating culture, community, and personal meaning in our schools.* San Francisco: Jossey-Bass.

Sinek, S. (2009, September). *How great leaders inspire action.* [Video file]. Retrieved from http://www.ted.com/talks/lang/en/simon_sinek_how_great_leaders_inspire_action.html

Sinek, S. (2010, July). Success takes help. *Re:Focus* [blog]. Retrieved from http://blog.startwithwhy.com/refocus/2010/07/success-takes-help.html

Sirota, D., Mischkind, L., & Meltzer, M. (2006, April 10). Why your employees are losing motivation. *Working Knowledge.* Cambridge, MA: Harvard Business School. Retrieved from http://hbswk.hbs.edu/archive/5289.html

Steiner, L. (2004). *Designing effective professional development experiences: What do we know?* Naperville, IL: Learning Point Associates.

Stern, D. S., Gerritz, W. H., & Little, J. W. (1989). Making the most of the district's two (or five) cents: Accounting for investments in teacher professional development. *Journal of Education Finance, 14*, 19–26.

Stillwell, R. (2010). *Public School Graduates and Dropouts From the Common Core of Data: School Year 2007–08* (NCES 2010-341). National Center for Education Statistics, Institute of Education Sciences, U.S. Department of Education. Washington, D.C. Retrieved from http://nces.ed.gov/pubsearch/pubsinfo .asp?pubid=2010341.

Stone, D., Patton, B., & Heen, S. (2000). *Difficult conversations*. New York: Penguin.

Success stories. (2012). *Dispelling the myth*. Washington, DC: Education Trust. Retrieved from http://www.edtrust.org/dc/resources/success-stories

Supovitz, J. (2001). Translating teaching practice into improved student achievement. In S. Fuhrman, (Ed.), *From the capitol to the classroom: Standards-based reforms in the states. The one hundredth yearbook of the National Society for the Study of Education, part two*, (pp. 81–98). Chicago: University of Chicago Press.

Swanson, C. (2010, June 10). U.S. graduation rate continues to decline. *Education Week*, 22–23, 30.

Thorndike, E. L. (1914). *Education: A first book*. New York: Macmillan.

Tschannen-Moran, M. (2004). *Trust matters: Leadership for successful schools*. San Francisco: Jossey-Bass.

Tyack, D., & Cuban, L. (1995). *Tinkering toward Utopia: A century of public school reform*. Cambridge, MA: Harvard University Press.

Tye, K. A. (1981.) *Changing our schools: The realities*. (Technical Report Series, No. 30). Los Angeles: Graduate School of Education, University of California Los Angeles.

U. S. Office of Special Education Programs. (2007). *History: Twenty-five years of progress educating children with disabilities through IDEA*. Washington, DC: Author. Retrieved from http://www2.ed.gov/policy/speced/leg/idea/history.html

Vulnerable (definition). (2011). In Merriam-Webster.com. Retrieved from http:// www.merriam-webster.com/dictionary/vulnerable

Waterman, R. H., & Peters, T. J. (1982). *In search of excellence*. New York: Harper Collins.

Wei, R. C., Darling-Hammond, L., & Adamson, F. (2010). *Professional development in the United States: Trends and challenges*. Dallas, TX: National Staff Development Council.

Wei, R. C., Darling-Hammond, L., Andree, A., Richardson, N., & Orphanos, S. (2009). *Professional learning in the learning profession: A status report on teacher development in the United States and abroad*. Dallas, TX: National Staff Development Council. Retrieved from http://srnleads.org/resources/ publications/nsdc.html

Wolk, R. (2009, April 22). Why we're still "at risk." *Education Week*, 30, 36.

Wright, S. P., Horn, S. P., & Sanders, W. L. (1997). Teacher and classroom context effects on student achievement: Implications for teacher evaluation. *Journal of Personnel Evaluation in Education, 11*(1), 57–67.

Yankelovich, D., & Friedman, W. (2011). *Toward wiser public judgment*. Nashville, TN: Vanderbilt University Press.

Yoon, K. S., Duncan, T., Lee, S. W.-L., Scarloss, B., & Shapley, K. (2007, October). *Reviewing the evidence on how teacher professional development affects student achievement.* (Issues & Answers Report, REL 2007—No. 33). Washington, DC: U.S. Department of Education, Institute of Education Sciences, National Center for Education Evaluation and Regional Assistance, Regional Educational Laboratory Southwest. Retrieved from http://nces.ed.gov/pubsearch/pubsinfo.asp?pubid=REL2007033

Zins, J. E., Bloodworth, M., Weissberg, R. P., & Walberg, H. J. (2004). *Building academic success on social and emotional learning: What does the research say?* New York: Teachers College Press.

Zinth, K. (2005, January). *State textbook adoption.* Denver, CO: Education Commission of the States. Retrieved from http://www.ecs.org/clearinghouse/57/75/5775.htm

Index

CORWIN
A SAGE Company

The Corwin logo—a raven striding across an open book—represents the union of courage and learning. Corwin is committed to improving education for all learners by publishing books and other professional development resources for those serving the field of PreK–12 education. By providing practical, hands-on materials, Corwin continues to carry out the promise of its motto: **"Helping Educators Do Their Work Better."**

Advancing professional learning for student success

Learning Forward (formerly National Staff Development Council) is an international association of learning educators committed to one purpose in K–12 education: Every educator engages in effective professional learning every day so every student achieves.

WITHDRAWAL